WHAT DOCTRINES TO EMBRACE

Studies in the History of American Education

Struggles to coerce uniformity of sentiment in support of some end thought essential to their time and country have been waged by many good as well as by evil men. Nationalism is a relatively recent phenomenon but at other times and places the ends have been racial or territorial security, support of a dynasty or regime, and particular plans for saving souls. As first and moderate methods to attain unity have failed, those bent on its accomplishment must resort to an ever increasing severity. As governmental pressure toward unity becomes greater, so strife becomes more bitter as to whose unity it shall be. Probably no deeper division of our people could proceed from any provocation than from finding it necessary to choose what doctrine and whose program public education officials shall compel youth to unite in embracing.

Justice Robert Jackson
West Virginia v. Barnette,
Majority Opinion (1943)

WHAT DOCTRINES TO EMBRACE

STUDIES IN THE HISTORY OF AMERICAN EDUCATION

CHARLES BURGESS

University of Washington

MERLE L. BORROWMAN

University of Wisconsin

KEYSTONES OF EDUCATION SERIES

ACADEMIC EDITORS

MERLE L. BORROWMAN, *University of Wisconsin*

ROBERT J. SCHAEFER, *Teachers College, Columbia University*

ISRAEL SCHEFFLER, *Harvard University*

EDWARD JOSEPH SHOBEN, JR., *American Council on Education*

SCOTT, FORESMAN AND COMPANY

The authors gratefully acknowledge permission of the
History of Education Quarterly and *Paedagogica Historica*
to reprint extended passages as follows:

From M. L. B., "False Dawn of the State University," in
History of Education Quarterly, I (June 1961): 6-22

From C. B., "William Maclure and Education for a Good
Society," in *History of Education Quarterly*,
III (June 1963): 58-76.

From C. B., "Two Tendencies of Educational Thought in
the New Nation," in *Paedagogica Historica*, IV (Ghent,
Belgium, 1964): 326-342 .

Library of Congress Catalog Card Number 77-78545

To Cora and Ellen

FOREWORD

The study of education is today in a state of ferment. With the expansion of educational horizons in American society, specialists of various sorts—historians, philosophers, psychologists, sociologists, political scientists—are to an ever greater extent joining with professional educators in inquiries into the nature of our educational ideas and institutions. Together, these scholars are enhancing the vitality, authority, and inspiration required of educational concepts in a revolutionary era of social change and scientific discovery.

In some small measure, the Keystones of Education Series is intended to reflect and, hopefully, to advance this educational development. It brings to instructors and students, indeed to all those concerned with education, a unique group of relatively brief but authoritative books, selective in content so as to develop in considerable depth key areas of knowledge. Each book is an original treatment of its special topic. The series may be profitably used in both introductory and advanced courses, for the instructor is free to construct a course with the content, emphasis, and sequence he desires, by selecting a combination of books to serve as text material. Because of the distinguished academic consultants and authorship, instructors can confidently take full advantage of the flexibility of the series without fear of uneven quality, superficiality, or duplication.

The Keystones of Education Series will for the first time make available a variety of superior materials, in convenient and inexpensive format, for the entire pre-service education program at colleges and universities.

The Publishers

TABLE OF CONTENTS

PREFACE

This volume in no way pretends to be a complete historical overview of American education. The following essays spring from our fascination with a few telling vignettes—a few of the more historically suggestive reflections cast by the many facets of American educational thought and practice since 1800.

Taken collectively, the following chapters depict a general chronological progression from 1800 to the present. Taken separately, each chapter should be perceived as an independent essay attempting to stop the movement of history momentarily and examine certain dominant interrelationships of various factors then impinging upon education. Selected individuals embroiled in educational ferment and change stand as symbols of their brief eras. Ranging from the Reverend Samuel Miller at the dawn of the federal period to James B. Conant in the middle decades of the twentieth century, these persons reify some of the major controversies raging over educational processes and community ideals in the United States.

Certain recurrent or persistent issues have incidentally given implicit continuity to these five essays: the relationship of the schools to the State and other social institutions, the struggles for the control of the educational system, competing concepts of human nature and the learning process, and the proliferation of "useful knowledge" and attendant strains on the curriculum. At times these issues have stood neat and tidy as fairly independent; usually, however, they have been twined about each other in a most exasperatingly typical manner.

In the fifth essay, dealing with the last forty years of educational history, our pursuit of these issues led us toward theoretical constructs in which neither the issues nor the individuals became dominant. Demographic and technological factors, which we generally ignored in chapters concerning rural and small-town America in the nineteenth century, assume a particularly dramatic quality with respect to twentieth-century urban American life. We have therefore attempted to relate these factors to the rhetoric of reform generated by and creating the popular issues of education.

In writing we have found the counsel of several fellow historians of immeasurable help. Although the authors bear responsibility for what follows, we will try to remember to share words of congratulation with our anonymous colleagues.

C. B.
M. L. B.

CHAPTER ONE

•

The Insidious Encroachments

of Innovation

•

*I have just heard with sorrow that [Jefferson] . . . has been chosen
President of the United States and Burr Vice-President. God grant us
patience to endure their tyranny! . . . The equality of the opinions of one
God, twenty Gods, or no God, is affirmed in Mr. Jefferson's "Notes on Virginia," and seems to be becoming the established creed.*
                                    THE REVEREND CHARLES NISBET
The advocates of the supremacy of Reason *and the* perfectibility
of Man, *at every successive retrospect of human affairs, will find themselves refuted and confounded.*
                                    THE REVEREND SAMUEL MILLER
*I did once flatter myself that the people of Tennessee would rally
around this infant seat of science [the nonsectarian University of Nash-
ville] . . . I did suppose that the good sense of the community would soon
perceive that a university cannot be in every town—that it must have some
one permanent location—and that, when once fixed and in operation, all
petty jealousies and rivalries would die away.*
                                    PHILIP LINDSLEY

Revolutionary America provided the utopian reformer the exhilarating and rare experience of speaking to inordinately large audiences. The great fact of American independence launched a remarkable outpouring of plans for the New Nation, plans political, social, economic, and educational. Historical experience could not be trusted to guide American destiny, it was asserted, save in a negative sense by providing countless examples of grotesque denials of human rights in the European "tradition." Americans were told that they must experiment. Failures there would be; but the desire and ability to sustain a dialogue with uncertainty would surely bring incalculable profit to mankind. All thoughtful plans, all experimental designs for developing an American character, then, should be considered and, if possible, tested in this hazardous venture into republicanism. Amid warnings only against the acceptance of ideas that might violate the "inherent and unalienable rights of man . . . ," those who hoped for steady national progress under the Federal Constitution did not forget to include educational reform as an item high in priority.[1]

By 1791, conditions for change in education were overripe. The American Revolution had dealt sharp blows to formal learning. College attendance had dropped markedly. Many schools became makeshift barracks, hospitals, and barns and were then abandoned. Others were destroyed. Little remained of the apprenticeship system of practical education. And too few Americans, it seemed, understood the danger of failing to restore, much less to improve upon, institutional education across the land. Still, in the face of the sizeable task ahead, hope ran high for at least the reawakening of dormant agencies of education. In some quarters, notably among New England Congregationalists, such hope expressed itself as a desire to restore learning patterns discernible in the prerevolutionary era. Those who drank deeply of the new republican spirits, however, accepted the disarray of the postrevolutionary years as a compelling challenge to erect new educational standards and goals suitable to men who had banked their collective future on the success of government-by-headcount. Among the general electorate, meanwhile, indifference to education ran high. Indeed, when it became apparent that most plans for "disseminating knowledge" depended upon support by general taxation, popular indifference often stiffened into outright opposition.

By 1800 it had already become commonplace to hear Americans immodestly call themselves "the most enlightened nation of the world." Even foreign visitors tolerantly noted a commendable degree of intelligence throughout the populace. But American leaders, conservative and reformer alike, disapproved of the ease

with which appeals to "common sense" came to imply that the value
of formal learning was at best questionable. Concerned patricians,
churchmen, yeomen, and artisans looked with a mixture of pride,
disbelief, and fear upon the newly liberated Common Man. Endowed with "common sense" or not, he sorely needed to be for-
mally educated.

Political democracy was at stake. Many articulate American
spokesmen agreed that the future of constitutional government in
the United States depended heavily upon vastly expanded educational opportunities for American youth. By no means did this
agreement mean that diverse political, religious, and economic
arguments were subsumed beneath a concerted attack upon ignorance. Political sparks continued to dance when Thomas Jefferson's
political views scraped against ideas thrust out by John Marshall,
but the two men found they could agree on the need for popular
education. Irreconcilable religious differences completely divided
the New England churchman Jedidiah Morse and freethinker
Joel Barlow, but they did not dispute the importance of formal
education. Even men of modest attainment, innocent of concern
for things speculative and forced to defend self-education as a
matter of self-respect if not of conviction, now and again came forward with pleas for public provision of learning. The shrewd New
England husbandman William Manning, himself struggling to
scratch legible and literate sentences in behalf of the rights of man,
insisted that "No person who is frind to Libberty will be against a
large expence in Larning."[2]

But this widespread verbal commitment to education seriously
misled any who thought it signaled rapid reform of education for
the masses. Debates on the proper role for education rumbled
through the new nation. They hinted of the emergence of two
major schools of educational thought. One school found telling
expression in the writings of such men as the Reverend Samuel
Miller of New York and Noah Webster of Massachusetts and was
particularly congenial to Calvinists and New England Federalists.
It served to round out the constitutional philosophy of John Adams
by suggesting, at least, the way in which his concept of the ideal
body politic could be transmitted to generations of Americans yet
unborn. It put the sharp bit of stern restraint into the mouth of the
American in what was taken to be his colt-like, cocksure quest of
happiness. It reminded him that happiness was a satanic device
to lure man into a denial of his innate and total depravity. According to this view, far better were it for man to accept the limitations
imposed upon him by Providence than to suffer from the curses of
pride and ambition that clung to the soul of him who forgot that:
"Yes, I was ever born in sin, And all my heart is bad within."

At the other pole, across the intervening welter of views regarding man and his education, an "enlightened" school of thought
looked for support to Thomas Jefferson and a host of allied spokesmen variously called "Republicans," "Deists," and "patriots" by
friendly voices, and "Jacobeans" and "Atheists" by their opponents.
The soil of the American revolution proved favorable to the growth
of enlightenment notions in the new nation. And with it grew a
faith in the power of education to create conditions for steady human progress. With education lay the best hope for the philosophy
of natural rights, for meliorism, the advance of science, and the
day when human reason would have won universal acclaim. With
a new shrillness after 1800 were heard cries not only for an extended program of popular education but for coeducation, equal
opportunities for all races, and an absolute separation of church
and state in educational processes. With uncommon heat it was
asserted further that no capricious Deity had planted in man's
breast sin, depravity, or servility; nor did He ever intervene in
human affairs. Rather He expected men to respect human reason,
to explore the unknown critically, and to spare no corner of human
concern from the light of inquiry even though others considered
the area in question to be sacrosanct.

Conservative political and religious forces launched a stern
counterattack against such "arrogant heresy." Ministers vigorously
lectured their parishioners to eschew and combat the twisted ideas
of the Enlightenment. The denial of depravity was declared to be
a madness in the land. In Sunday sermons, pamphlets, and political orations, respected spokesmen inveighed against the malaise of
such irreligion which, some insisted, was being supported in this
country by secret agents of revolutionary France. Other conservatives, after carefully reexamining the dark caverns of the human
mind, returned to report that enlightenment optimism about the
improvability of human nature not only lacked foundation but cut
away at the interests of sound government.

The inheritance of colonial patterns of thought and behavior
stubbornly resisted liberal theories of change in the spirit of revolution and Enlightenment. General accord about the need for education, therefore, placed only a fragile crust of common ground atop
quicksands of deep-seated differences. The greatest questions
seemed most unresolvable. Would education be viewed as the
brake of social restraint and restoration or the accelerator of reconstruction according to enlightenment postulates? The "what"
and "how" of education were firmly trapped in the web of ideological disputes.

The New England colonial idea of tribal community welded
by bonds of religious affection and guided by a consensus of virtue

among tribal leaders continued to stir in the heart of Congregationalists in the early 1800's. Eager as they were to accept the promises of the new century as Americans as well as New Englanders, the Congregationalists and Presbyterians still looked wistfully to their unfulfilled dream of community solidarity. Their understanding of human nature made them skeptical of the widely heralded free and common man. Their concern for work, duty, and perseverence heightened their antagonism to incipient social laissez-faire. A creature of sin, the man beyond community encouragement—and censure—would prove to be a malevolent creature. For man's own good, and for the glory of God, the community served as the chief agency of restraint, control, and guidance. Such traditional ideas as these needed a second and fairer trial, especially in the light of the establishment of constitutional government. The warning given by Jedidiah Morse, a highly respected spokesman of conservatism, was to be heard in countless addresses by fellow conservatives. "Let us guard against the insidious encroachments of *innovation* . . . , that evil and beguiling spirit which is now stalking to and fro through the earth, seeking whom he may destroy."[3]

Innovation, a mild word to describe the ideas championed by Elihu Palmer and his deistic circle, represented with considerable accuracy the ends pursued by many Jeffersonian democrats. Accepting the spirit of the assertion "that all men are created equal," believing that man's innate moral sense destroyed all argument for his depravity, and firm in a faith that happiness, be it found in much property or peace of mind, could only be pursued in the absence of local and national restraints, "innovators" had no patience for millenial visions of American communities organized in a neopuritan pattern. They substituted a vision of their own and called it Progress. The human community should serve to liberate man from the bondage of ignorance. Rather than act as an agency of restraint, the community should serve as a check on all desires to restrain man. Given a basic education in literacy and calculations, man in his goodness would grow over a lifetime of continued self-education and his certain contributions to a free society would bring incalculable benefits to generations yet unborn. Given these conditions, reformers flatly asserted, each man could be trusted to work out his own destiny and to raise the quality of social existence at the same time. In speech and song, therefore, reformers heralded the 1801 presidential inauguration of Thomas Jefferson as a double triumph. First, many of "Columbia's sons," choosing to ignore the narrow squeak of Jefferson's victory, expected now to see a great wave of "innovations" designed to make liberty forever secure. Second, they noted with alacrity that the nation had repudiated John Adams and his "Alien and Sedition Laws" at the close of his first term of office. The Star was in the East, all signs were clear, and in rousing manner the victors sang of the end of Adams and the beginning of a new century of Progress:

> The gloomy night before us flies,
> The reign of terror now is o'er;
> Its gags, inquisitors and spies,
> Its herds of harpies are no more.
> Rejoice, Columbia's sons, rejoice;
> To tyrants never bend the knee,
> But join with heart and soul and voice
> For Jefferson and liberty.

No dramatic changes in educational opportunities for the common man were to be forthcoming for nearly a generation in the face of these deep ideological divisions. But against the idea of the community as a bridle to control mischievous man, meanwhile, grew the idea of malleable man living in freedom of such undue restraint. In opposition to the notion of man assigned to fixed stations in this life rose the notion of man's natural equality. And in increasing numbers Americans came to believe that faith in human reason, equality, and the perfectibility of man and his institutions was justifiable and linked inseparably to universal education. While the seeds of educational reform were in gestation, the debates about whether they would produce weeds to be destroyed or plants deserving cultivation were instructive to an uncertain nation.

I

SAMUEL MILLER OF NEW YORK CITY

Federalists found little reason to greet the turn of a new century with rejoicing in 1801. Deeply distressed at the course of union in its unsteady first dozen years, they faced the grim prospect of contending with Jefferson as President of the United States for the next four years at least. Not only had the seat of national government slipped from Philadelphia, the London of America, to the swamps near Virginia, but the most radical equalitarian from that most populous state now held the reins of national destiny. Then as now, bad news traveled fast. "I have just heard with sorrow," wrote the respected Presbyterian clergyman Charles Nisbet on December 16, 1800, that Jefferson "has been chosen President of the United States, and Burr Vice-President. God grant us patience to endure their tyranny!"[4]

Nisbet, whose reputation as a divine enabled him to serve out his days as president of Dickinson College in Pennsylvania, was not alone in believing that the election of Jefferson ushered in the last but most dangerous days of the age of the Enlightenment in America. In a letter to the Reverend Samuel Miller of New York City, Nisbet declared the most distinguishing characteristic of the enlightenment to be

> the *spirit of free inquiry*, which has been so prominent, and which indeed has been carried almost to madness. I was born in the thirty-sixth year of it, when it was rather past its vigour; and, of late, when it seems to be past child-bearing, it teems with the most monstrous and mis-shapen productions. Air-Balloons; the Rights of Man; the Sovereignty of the People; and [Nisbet added, with a hint of the suspected French origin of all these aberrations] the Guillotine, are the productions of its dotage and decreptitude. And as old people are twice children, the present age, in the progress of decreptitude, is busy in vamping up old publications, and reviving old exploded errors, such as Atheism, Socinianism, and what seems the last stage of delirium, the indifference to all opinions in religion. The equality of the opinions of one God, twenty Gods, or no God, is affirmed in Mr. Jefferson's "Notes on Virginia," and seems to be becoming the established creed.[5]

Samuel Miller readily accepted Nisbet's analysis of the implications of "the *spirit of free inquiry*." It mirrored the solemn judgment shared by Jedidiah Morse, Timothy Dwight, Fisher Ames, and a host of respected leaders of Federalism. Profoundly distrustful of the "common people," alarmed to note that the rights of man had widely supplanted concern for the duties of man, these conservatives rallied to insist that the extension of individual liberty be delayed until all citizens could be properly educated in the moral principles of Protestantism. Many churches sensed the need for evangelical revivalism, one that called for an army of modern Jonathan Edwardses and George Whitefields. Americans had to be educated in literacy, to be sure; but above all else, they needed to learn moral restraint as taught in the scriptures, particularly in the Old Testament.

A humane man who publicly opposed slavery and supported education, Miller at the same time set himself against promoters of the notion that education should be secular in both content and control. Yet as a member of the American Philosophical Society he was aware of the esteem accorded to such notions by Americans of high influence. Between 1795 and 1797 the Society had conducted an essay contest "on certain specific subjects of useful Education," which not only drew enthusiastic response but also gave added weight to Miller's fears of mounting national irreligiosity. In 1797 the Society judged that a joint award should be made to the Reverend Samuel Knox of Maryland and Samuel H. Smith, a twenty-five-year-old Philadelphia journalist, both of whom argued in their separate essays for a national system of education and against parochial and private education. Knox's well-phrased plea was for a "*uniform system of national education*" based "*on principles of the most extensive utility.*" Smith not only echoed this view, he especially urged that such public instruction be compulsory. In order to render "the prevalence of virtue . . . secure by the diffusion of useful knowledge," Smith further argued that his proposed national university, as the capstone of American public education, be presided over by a scientist, not by a minister.[6]

That the essay contest sponsored by the American Philosophical Society sprang from a growing patrician concern for the education of American youth probably gratified Samuel Miller. But that the award should have gone to Smith and Knox was tantamount to a direct attack upon Miller and his colleagues in conservatism. That the Society so eagerly embraced enlightenment postulates, as revealed in the emphasis Smith and Knox placed upon science, reason, human progress, and equality, was indeed cause for deep concern.

For such a thoughtful and influential Presbyterian minister as Miller, therefore, it was not enough to prepare the customary New Year's sermon in January 1801. More than a new year had arrived; 1801 had launched a new century, one fraught with more perils than promise for the United States. In a series of Sunday sermons, and eventually in careful essays, Miller incisively summarized the broad social, political, educational, and economic changes of the last century and eloquently expressed his hopes and fears for the course of American life in the new, the nineteenth, century. In 1803 his views reached beyond his circle of attentive New York City parishioners to wider audiences when printed in a two-volume study titled *A Brief Retrospect of the Eighteenth Century.*[7]

If only for its excellent statement of puritan opposition to educational ideas fundamental to "enlightened" reformers, the *Brief Retrospect* made an important contribution to American thought. Miller's volume nowhere revealed more fully his guarded optimism for the new century than in its chapters on education. As was to be expected, Miller warned that it was not enough merely to press for the extension of educational opportunities in the years ahead. Education, admittedly a central issue of national concern, needed to be understood as a problem for churchmen. Anxious to chart the course of educational reform himself, Miller warned against the ideals of those leaders in the movement for educational reform who accepted the un-Christian doctrine of human perfectibility.

"Philosophers of the Nineteenth Century!" he pleaded, learn caution and wisdom from "the mistakes of those deluded and presumptuous spirits who have misled and corrupted their species. . . !" Only the doctrine of total depravity, in harmony with the nature and condition of man through all human experience, stood on Christian principles. "The sacred volume teaches us that we are fallen and depraved beings; that this depravity is total . . . ; that the most virtuous will never be perfect or completely holy in the present world, and that misery and death are the unavoidable lot of man while under the present dispensation."[8]

By ascribing to education "a kind of intellectual and moral *omnipotence*," many Christians, Miller believed, swallowed the barbed hook of deism. They became unwitting agents for the philosophy of the cloven hoof. Christians who in blind enthusiasm applauded education as an all-powerful engine of reform stood only a short step away from acceptance of the entire enlightenment syllogism. They soon found themselves parroting the delusive notion that to education could be ascribed the major "talents, and dispositions of men; and that by improving its principles and plan, human nature may, and finally will, reach a state of absolute perfection in this world, or at least go on to a state of unlimited improvement." Miller conceded that education was "extremely powerful" and that "useful reforms in the plans of instruction" might greatly "promote the general improvement of man."[9] But it seemed to Miller that American reformers went far beyond his "reasonable" views. For the doctrine of human perfectibility played seductively upon man's pride, with promises of a heaven on earth. In due course, however, it would surely dash its followers upon the rocks of human vanity and leave them for eternity as shipwrecked souls. Miller and his conservative colleagues were one in their belief that the doctrine of perfectibility ("too pregnant with mischief" and with considerable currency in "many parts of the civilized world") was a sinister legacy from the eighteenth century. To teachers, ministers, and educational theorists of the nineteenth century fell the task of stemming the force of enlightenment doctrines and their influence upon American minds.[10]

Miller's *Brief Retrospect* made it clear that the course for the extension of educational opportunities had to be charted along Christian lines. In addition to reporting the trends in education observable in 1803 Miller offered specific countermeasures to enlightenment ideas. He attacked the "softness" of current pedagogical theories and practices and alluded to Rousseau's *Emile* as immoral and impracticable.[11] He gave grudging approval of the admission of new and utilitarian studies to the curriculum, while lamenting that "the greater number of scholars, at the present day, are more remarkable for *variety* than *depth* of learning . . . ."[12] The declining prestige of Latin and Greek studies represented a double danger according to the *Brief Retrospect*. First, it revealed an overweening penchant for utility, which was grave error enough; but this penchant for utility created an even greater second danger: It worked to the ultimate benefit of enlightenment doctrinaires. "To recommend the dismission of classic literature . . . from plans of education, is not only to declare war against taste and sound learning," Miller charged, "but also to betray the interests of evangelical truth, and put a new weapon into the hands of its enemies."[13]

Inveighing against the spread of coeducation and the educational implications of feminist views spread by followers of Mary Wollstonecraft, a famous British peddlar of progress, Miller insisted that to break the sex barrier in education and employment would "be productive of the most *immoral consequences*." A good puritan, Miller knew that the evil seed within each lad's breast grew uncontrollably when in protracted company with equally sinful females. He threw off all restraint in describing probable fruits of such union. Coeducation would have the general effect of undoing civilization. In its particular effects coeducation "would convert society into hordes of seducers and prostitutes. Instead of . . . the pure delights of wedded love, a system of universal concubinage would prevail." Even worse, "Seminaries of learning would be changed into nurseries of licentiousness and disease; the proceedings of deliberative assemblies would be perverted or arrested by the wiles of amorous intrigue; the places of commercial or mechanical business would become the haunts of noisy and restless lewdness; and all sober employment would yield to the dominion of brutal appetite."[14]

Every alert reader of the *Brief Retrospect* who played guilt-by-association games could have been expected to see coeducationists as orgiastic hedonists and to see in "reform" a conspiracy against the truth of man's condition as a depraved creature ever in need of policing. Miller left no doubt that he saw the ideological battle-lines drawn in the nineteenth century between human perfectibility and human depravity. Apparently radical ideas from such British agitators as William Godwin and from French extremists Helvetius and Condorcet had infiltrated the Jeffersonian ranks in the United States. Thus transformed, Jeffersonianism sought to reeducate the nation in the ways of human perfectibility. Miller was more oblique, temperate, and respectable than many of his conservative allies in coming to this conclusion. He was no protean McCarthyite like fellow churchman Jedidiah Morse who, a few years earlier, had announced the presence of *"secret societies,* under the influence and direction of France" in the United States. "I have now in my possession," Morse declared, "complete and indubitable proof that such societies do exist, and have for many years existed. . . . I have, my brethren, an official, authenticated list of the names, ages, places of nativity, professions, &c. of the officers and members of a Society of Illuminati . . . constituting of *one hundred* members, instituted in Virginia, by the *Grand Orient* of France." [15]

Miller's *Brief Retrospect* gave little direct support to windmill-raiders like Morse. Miller was content to assert that Jeffersonians were puffed up with delusions of man's natural goodness and capacity to reason his way to indefinite if not infinite perfectibility. They simply could not see that educational reform had to proceed along lines dictated by Protestant religion. And obviously they were incapable of serving the highest interests of the nation. True educational reform, concluded Miller, had to spring from sound theological premises and possess a program broad enough to obviate sectarian disputes.

Thus could truly Christian patterns of thought and behavior be reinstated in America under the aegis of the church. Before the nineteenth century would have run its course, Miller prophesied, "The advocates of the *supremacy of Reason* and the *perfectibility of Man,* at every successive retrospect of human affairs, will find themselves refuted and confounded." [16] Eternal Truths would once more be unchallenged as guiding principles for preachers, professors, and politicians. To this end Miller expressed the hope that, especially for laboring classes and "indigent portions of society," the safely orthodox Sunday School movement would soon gain general acceptance throughout the Christian world. [17] Or, better indeed to sustain the old order in education for the present, and keep the school under the watchful eye of the local church than to expand educational opportunities under the spell of Jeffersonianism.

Even as Miller spoke in praise of the Sunday School movement, however, it was becoming less an agency to promote the 3 R's than to advance the cause of sectarian Protestanism. Few considered it a likely candidate to spearhead a national program of education. Among other novel plans the Lancastrian or monitorial movement was soon to enjoy a modest vogue, largely because it could train large numbers of students inexpensively, a distinct virtue. DeWitt Clinton worked diligently in behalf of this British plan for the mass education of youth and made his—and Miller's—home state of New York a national pace-setter in Lancastrianism. But in addition to the system's failure to consider the "individual differences" to which modern educational psychology pays such careful attention, monitorial learning failed on two other counts. First it bore the stigma of being devised to train "the lower classes," and Americans with their freshly won freedoms and great social mobility were little inclined to lend sustained support to class education, however low the cost. Second, its applicability was limited to large communities and remained unsuited to the needs of an essentially rural America. Joseph Cabell, one of the founders of the University of Virginia, was not alone in questioning the utility of a system that assumed the American landscape to have been dominated by large towns. Did Lancastrianism, asked Cabell, offer any solution to the needs of "small Country Schools"?[18] Obviously not. With the singular exception of the flurry of interest stirred by monitorial schools, however, free and common education for American youth made painfully slow progress in the first quarter of the nineteenth century. "Planters, merchants, and professional men everywhere preferred to manage the education of their own children in their own way and to leave that of the less fortunate to church and charity."[19]

Colleges, however, received impressive, tangible benefits from this early interest in education. Where the interests of reformers as well as conservatives were directed toward education, colleges proliferated. Led by Presbyterians, Congregationalists, and Methodists, churchmen especially worked mightily to promote higher education. At this level of learning it seemed that secularism, science, and other "enlightened" postulates had made startling inroads. Assuming that national leaders would continue to be drawn heavily from the college-bred community, churchmen were determined that such a community be motivated by religious certitudes in the service of religious ends. The alarming news of irreligiosity and atheism on the western frontiers further contributed to the growth of colleges. More church colleges across the land, it was reasoned, would serve both as a measure to increase the size of the missionary armies and to provide an indigenous college-trained ministry in the heathen-breeding hinterlands. Conservative churchmen had little sympathy for the Jeffersonian assertion that unless colleges were rooted in a system of universal and free common schools they would create such a gulf between an ignorant populace and a learned patrician class as to imperil, if not destroy, constitutional government. Conservatives such as Noah Webster believed that insofar as Jeffersonians equated "constitutional government" with "democracy" such a political transformation would be desirable. The need for more colleges remained unchallenged as the first order of educational business for American churches. In an 1820 address before professors and supporters of higher education Webster restated this widely shared belief. "Blessed be *our* lot! We live to see a new era in the history of man—an era when reason and religion begin to resume their sway, and to impress the heavenly truth, that the appropriate business of men, is to imitate the Savior; to serve their God; and bless their fellow men. . . . No, my friends; the man who loves the peace and security *in this life*, must lend his aid to the propagation of the gospel. . . . The *gospel* only can convert swords into ploughshares and spears into pruning hooks—the gospel only can supersede the necessity of bolts and bars—the gospel only can dispeople the state prison and the penitentiary!"[20]

In their fight to restore traditional patterns of intellectual life and denominational leadership to the nation, churchmen established over five hundred colleges by 1861. More than eighty per cent of them foundered, but the record of zeal with which churches stalked the spectre of secular scientism from Washington, D.C., to the wilderness was most impressive. Between 1799 and 1830 alone, ignoring the many ill-begotten institutions that quickly withered and died, the sects established twenty-four new colleges in America. In that brief period they came within one college of matching the total number of permanent colleges established over the course of nearly two hundred years of colonial experience.[21]

In this sphere Samuel Miller's hopes for the future refutation of "the *supremacy of Reason* and the *perfectibility of Man*, at every successive retrospect of human affairs," came closest to full realization. Academic freedom, a *sine qua non* of higher education for holders of "enlightened" values, suffered a sharp if short-lived setback. Even the noted Harvard professor George Ticknor, who fought so effectively for a more flexible college curriculum, held academic freedom in low esteem. Ticknor held that academic freedom led to skepticism in religion and irresponsibility in politics. For him too, the spirit of free inquiry ate away at social unity; and Ticknor considered it fortunate that public opinion in the United States forced conformity of thought in academe.[22] With small denominational colleges leading the way, there set in what has been called a "Great Retrogression" away from freedom of thought and inquiry in higher education between 1800 and 1830.[23] The sciences had first to be twisted into alignment with accepted Biblical truths before they could enlist denominational college support.

Resistance to secular purposes in higher education, however, had roots in positive community ideals. Town fathers guarded the delicate web of common moral sanctions in their community. They personally policed the local school and other tribal agencies in order to perpetuate regnant ideals. But every young man who packed his trunk for a distant college risked peril for himself and, assuming that he returned, for his home town as well. Would he be instructed in the accepted virtues, be seduced by a competing religious creed, or worse, fall prey to a spiritually indifferent celebration of free inquiry? Not if the community could either mount its own collegiate program or, through alliances with like-minded communities in the region, send its youth to a college that truly functioned *in loco parentis.* Opponents of free inquiry thus tended to confirm Ticknor's views. Higher education should elevate communal ideals as a system of truth superior to individual human reason; colleges should make knowledge serve tribal moral imperatives; colleges should inspire community stability rather than promote potentially disruptive change in the name of Progress.

Was there no place for the idea that knowledge could be moral without explicitly serving sectarian purposes? Or no place for an institution of higher learning supported by the state and charged to promote interests common to all communities? One believing there was such a place had to face certain disquieting prospects. A state-supported scholarly community would probably bear no close resemblance to any other community within the state. Such a scholarly community would necessarily be nonsectarian or secular; it would in all probability become a sanctuary for views that would, from time to time, prove threatening to town fathers in every community served by the state institution.

It fell to the few—to such men as Jefferson, Horace Holley, Thomas Cooper, and Philip Lindsley—to support a more liberal, secular, and scientific higher education. As these men were to discover, their conception of a community of scholars placed them at odds with sectarianism and home-town values everywhere. The attempts of Cooper, Holley, and Lindsley to establish collegiate programs uncolored by denominationalism in any form were fated to become especially unhappy episodes in American higher education during the early nineteenth century.

II

THOMAS COOPER AT SOUTH CAROLINA COLLEGE

South Carolina College was in many respects a unique—hence suspect—institution in the era of the Great Retrogression. Here was provided a curriculum which, though limited, gave a major place to modern languages, science, and political economy. Ironically enough, the first major curriculum change was the extension of classical studies. The irony inheres in the fact that such a change was forced on the college by its president, Thomas Cooper, a scientist and political economist whose secularist attitude toward knowledge made him anathema to those very sectarian groups which tended to support the classical curriculum. The battle between secularism and dogmatism at South Carolina College was among the first and most violent in the war that swept higher education throughout most of the nineteenth century. In this battle, which Cooper lost despite his labors for the classics, the college battlefield was reduced to ruins; the standard histories of the college blame Cooper for destroying it between 1821 and 1823.

Cooper was the sort of man who defied classification. A lover of liberty, forced to leave England under charges of treason because of his machinations with the leaders of the French Revolution, and imprisoned for sedition in the United States because of his criticism of John Adams, Cooper penned some of the most eloquent essays on the natural inferiority of Negroes and the natural justice of black slavery. Ever, or almost ever, the great apostle of freedom of the press and speech, he encouraged the censorship of abolitionist literature. A great friend of the mass, in the abstract, he could not tolerate living with the common man in person. An arch anti-Federalist, he conspired to place Nicholas Biddle in the White House. Cooper was the author of highly scholarly and closely reasoned volumes in political economy, law, medicine, and chemistry, but was given to hysterical exaggeration and innuendo in public controversy. As is so frequently the case, those who defended the man on principle often found his action indefensible.[24]

Cooper's opponents invariably appeared to him as Presbyterians, or as some other kind of bigoted Calvinist, with a dismal distrust of human reason and a completely irrational commitment to primitive superstition, to which they were determined to enslave mankind. His opponents charged that he was almost insanely obsessed. In the words of one of them: "These clergymen are sadly in the old gentleman's way. Whether he writes a book on Political Economy, a metaphysical tract on free enquiry—whether he is treating of Geology or Chemistry—the Clergy—the Clergy still elbow him. They are like Hamlet's ghost;—he shifts his ground, but with ghostly pertinacity, they still haunt him. If he rides upon a highway, they confront his path—in the streets they attend him— and at every corner he comes—pop upon them;—until terrified by his own fancies, and in the warmth of his imagination, the very posts and old trees are converted into Clergymen."[25]

It is true that Cooper saw clergymen everywhere. He was certain that they sought control of all educational institutions.

The schools they could not control, they would, he believed, destroy by the charge of "godlessness." But the clergymen he saw were not all ghosts. At the University of Virginia the Presbyterians blocked his appointment as professor, though Jefferson had supported him. At South Carolina College, where people from many denominations lived together in harmony and tolerance, prayers were enforced twice daily and attended by the faculty, including Cooper; but several congressional investigations were called for at the insistence of the Presbyterians. These investigations failed to produce evidence that Cooper or any other faculty member had used his position to attack any religious group. Almost invariably students testified that Cooper urged them to support the religion of their families. Within the College itself there was, then, little religious tension during Cooper's regime. From the outside, however, the clergy mounted continuous attacks.

In 1822, shortly after Cooper became president, the legislature appointed a committee to investigate Presbyterian charges that discipline at the College was deteriorating because of the president's sceptical attitude toward religion. Cooper was cleared, and even the legislative committee wondered if the grand juries initiating the investigation had not lent themselves to "the purposes of sectarian zeal."[26]

Thus, for all practical purposes, was Cooper's presidency begun; thus was it to end. In the intervening years neither Cooper nor the sectarians missed many opportunities to press the attack. That Cooper's translation of J. V. S. Broussais' "On Irritation and Insanity" should enter largely into the final conflict supports the thesis that opposition between secular and nonsecular canons of knowledge was critical. Cooper hailed the Frenchman as a leading exponent of physiological medicine and materialism who produced secular theories of human nature at odds with those promulgated by dogmatic religion.

Along with the Broussais translation Cooper republished several of his own materialistic essays written during an earlier controversy with the Pennsylvania clergy. Cooper's essays "proved," according to him, and "sacreligiously charged," according to his enemies, that concepts of human nature based on metaphysical speculation and revealed religion were destined to become obsolete. As if this were not offensive enough, Cooper had added the further damnable argument that Jesus himself was a materialist. Clearly, no compromise was possible; another investigation of Cooper's regime came to pass in 1831 and 1832.

Once again, Cooper's friends in the legislature and on the board of trustees secured his clearance; but he was, in fact, defeated. The College had been thoroughly discredited and was no longer accepted by many South Carolinians. Enrollments fell alarmingly, discipline problems increased, and, on November 27, 1833, Cooper resigned the presidency of the College. A year later he resigned his professorship.

According to Daniel Walker Hollis, the University's official biographer, Cooper had so shaken the public's faith in the institution that hostility still remains in many quarters:

> Cooper's career at the College ultimately did much to bring about the founding of denominational colleges and the fragmentation of the state's efforts to provide higher education. His forays into religious and political fields injected the college into public affairs and this, too, has been to its detriment. The reaction to Cooper also contributed to increasing parochialism in South Carolina: Henceforth the State was more suspicious of and hostile to intellectual immigrants, and less tolerant of those who disagreed with prevailing dogma.[27]

After Cooper's resignation the power of organized religion grew rapidly in the state, and only when the College was safely in the hands of such pillars of orthodoxy as Robert Barnwell and the Reverend James H. Thornwell did it begin to recover public support. No doubt they were intelligent and tolerant men who did much for the College—indeed Thornwell, at least, had been a student of Cooper's—but the era which they dominated was very different from that which preceded it. Leaders of organized religion were consciously courted, and the kind of speculation concerning human nature that Cooper had conducted was passé.

In 1845 Thornwell thought of resigning the critically important Professorship of Sacred Literature and Evidences of Christianity which he had been given shortly after Cooper's resignation. President Preston, the source of whose apprehensions is evident, wrote the Charleston Presbytery, "We cannot afford to lose Doctor Thornwell from the College. In the first place he is the representative of the Presbyterian Church, which embraces the bone and sinew of the state, without whose support the institution cannot exist."[28]

Hollis describes Thornwell as struggling manfully to defend the doctrine that man is incurably evil. He had, says Hollis, "nothing but scorn for the 'heretical' doctrines that exalted the excellence of human nature and the perfectibility of man."[29] Thornwell did not consider the college an agency for social reform. Its job, he maintained, was to preserve the social order. To be sure, he did speak out on social issues, defending slavery and excoriating abolitionists in a manner that would have delighted his old teacher Thomas Cooper. But one scarcely wonders where that old Jacobin and Deist would have placed himself in the world described by Thornwell as made up of "atheists, socialists, communists, red republicans, and Jacobins on the one side, and the friends of order and regulated freedom on the other. In a word," said he, "the world is the battleground—Christianity and atheism the combatants; and the progress of humanity the stake."[30]

One problem remains. The College of South Carolina was established in the era of Revolutionary optimism, and a great deal of Jeffersonian sympathy still existed when Cooper assumed its presidency. Yet evangelical religion was already on the march, and Cooper's religious views were at sharp variance with those of most South Carolinians. Always quarrelsome and intemperate in argument, his reputation as a trouble-maker was well established before he appeared in Columbia. How did he survive so long?

Perhaps the answer lies partly in his undisputed distinction as a scholar in law, medicine, chemistry, and political economy— fields which the American community was finding increasingly valuable. Moreover, Cooper was a vigorous exponent of states' rights, free trade, and slavery—views held by most of his constituency. As one of the first to suggest that the time had come when South Carolina should "calculate the value of the Union," Cooper endeared himself to a growing group of "nullifiers," though he offended the strong union sentiment that still existed. The problem was one of balance of power. The sectarians could not alone defeat the coalition of secularists, free traders, states' rightists, and radicals who supported Cooper in his early years. But the strength of his opponents grew, and by 1830 a coalition of pro-unionists and evangelical religionists controlled the legislature in which the final charges against Cooper were brought.

By the time the actual hearings were held the nullifiers had gained ascendancy, and Cooper, whom they viewed as a near martyr to their cause, was briefly saved. However, greater unanimity on political issues was rapidly developing. Cooper's obnoxious religious views needed no longer to be tolerated when his support on political issues was no longer required. When no ideological group is powerful enough to control a state government, the elective or appointive board of control may safeguard critical inquiry at a university, if only because it cannot agree on whose dogma to follow. The same kind of a board, however, may become useless for this purpose when ideological unanimity develops in the community. In such times orthodoxy, ever the enemy of the secular spirit, governs the state university. Even if the board resists, as it did for a time in South Carolina, a public which insists on dogmatic answers may destroy a university that refuses to support these answers.

Two men destined to become casualties in the struggle to establish a new kind of higher education had visited Monticello in 1818 and sought the advice of Thomas Jefferson. One, Thomas Cooper, was hoping for a professorship in the new University of Virginia. As we have noted this was a vain hope; the sectarians had already identified him as an enemy. The second, young Horace Holley, fresh from religious controversies in New England, was en route to Lexington to consider the presidency of Transylvania University. Both shared many of Jefferson's opinions about higher education and received encouragement from him; both were to fight the same conservative forces that made Jefferson's struggles for the University of Virginia difficult.

Transylvania traced its origins back to the action of the Virginia Legislature, which in 1780 had donated 8,000 acres of escheated land to promote seminaries of learning in the western country. In 1783 Transylvania Seminary had been chartered under a self-perpetuating board. Only the tender care and zeal of the Presbyterians kept this struggling school alive through the succeeding decades. Had they been more careful (or less tolerant) in appointing subsequent members of the controlling board, Transylvania might have remained merely one of their many denominational colleges. In time, however, the Presbyterians found themselves in a minority position on the board that appointed a Unitarian minister as head of the seminary.

Stung by this event, the Presbyterians withdrew from Transylvania and started to build a competing denominational academy. For this they, too, received a legislative grant of 6,000 acres of public lands. Before their new Kentucky Academy could begin operation, however, Transylvania was in the hands of a respected Episcopalian minister, James Moore. Since the Presbyterians had complete confidence in Moore, a union of the two schools was in order. In 1799 the newly enlarged Transylvania University was chartered by the legislature of Kentucky. Interestingly enough, the Presbyterians were again in control of its governing board.

Through brief periods of sectarian harmony, or complete Presbyterian dominance, the fortunes of the University began to improve. There were established, and sporadically operated, departments of law and medicine, in addition to the expanded academic department. By 1815, however, religious conflict was again rife, and the legislature threatened to replace the self-perpetuating board with an elective one. Too late to prevent this action, two Presbyterian board members joined the liberal minority to elect Horace Holley as president. In spite of this, the legislature dismissed the board and appointed a new one which included no clerical members. From this new board Holley accepted appointment in 1818.

According to James Hopkins, the historian of Kentucky University, "the revolution against sectarianism had succeeded, the liberals were in control, and the Presbyterians began the organization of another college, Centre, which should be theirs only."[31] According to the Presbyterian viewpoint, "From that time, with an unGodly board and a Unitarian President, that institution [Transylvania] sent forth infidel graduates with great uniformity."[32]

Holley had been assured of state financial support by the governor and by leading legislators. The congregations of Lexington, even the Presbyterian congregation, had bid him welcome. Writing to his wife he promised happiness in Lexington: "We shall be more independent than we have ever been, and modes of influence will be opened to us, which we could not enjoy at the head of a parish merely, in any country. It is much better to be a rallying point for all the sects, than to be the partisan of either, however powerful that sect might be. But no sect in this country can swallow up the others. They must continue to check and balance each other, and to leave wise men an opportunity for safe and full inquiry."[33]

For nine years the promise of success and happiness was realized. Modern languages, political economy, history, pharmacy, surveying, navigation, and the natural sciences received a respected place in the college curriculum, beside the classical languages, mathematics, and philosophy. One of the nation's leading medical faculties was assembled, and a law school, short-lived to be sure, was started. Perhaps little credit is due Holley for the pioneering natural history research and teaching carried out by the brilliant Constantine S. Rafinesque, since Holley and Rafinesque did not get along particularly well, but it is significant that Transylvania, under Holley, did provide a place for such new research.

In a few short years Transylvania began to attract favorable attention throughout the nation, and her enrollment grew rapidly. The state of Kentucky provided sizeable financial grants which were augmented by gifts from the city of Lexington and private individuals. Unfortunately, none of these sources was dependable or regular enough for Holley to feel secure. Even in the years of glory Transylvania lived a hand-to-mouth existence, never knowing whether its outstretched hand would be refilled.

To the more extreme sectarians Holley continued to appear a dangerously deistic heretic; to back-country fundamentalists and anti-intellectuals he was a snob addicted to the near-sinful habits of high society. His personal manners were too fine; the use of wines, the Sunday evening musicales, his attendance at horse races, even the seminude sculpture in his home were exaggerated and excoriated. Only in Lexington were he and his wife Mary deeply respected. Indeed, the Lexington newspapers refused to print attacks upon him.

But Lexington itself, whose polite society took pride in having built a new Athens on the frontier, was thought by the back-country folk to be the seat of a degenerate and grasping aristocracy. Transylvania became a symbol—of high culture to Lexingtonians, of degeneracy and aristocracy to those in the rural areas. By 1825 an agrarian sense of economic exploitation was in league with the forces of religious fundamentalism and frontier anti-intellectualism against Lexington and Holley. With the Jacksonian Democrats and the religious fundamentalists in firm control of the state government, the future of Transylvania was bleak. Holley resigned in March 1827; within a year he was dead. In the early years of the 1820's, one might have guessed that Kentucky was ready for a modern state university. In retrospect it is clear that a small minority, advanced in their views of education, had but temporarily controlled the state and given Holley a few brief years of opportunity. The events leading to his resignation and the subsequent decline of Transylvania are evidence that the larger public of Kentucky had never accepted these views or this institution as their own.

When the Morrill Act of 1862 gave Kentucky a chance to establish a university more clearly designed to serve the interests of farmers and mechanics, her people once more attempted a compromise between a sectarian and a public secular system. By this time Transylvania was virtually in ruin. Its facilities were merged with those of Kentucky University, a Disciples of Christ college. Once again opposition developed among the Baptists, Methodists, and Presbyterians, who accused the Disciples of Christ of having used state resources to further their own sectarian ends. New conflicts, as bitter as those of the Holley era, followed before a university that was entirely controlled by the state came into being.

PHILIP LINDSLEY AND THE UNIVERSITY OF NASHVILLE

That the Presbyterians became the bitter enemies of Cooper and Holley is a tribute to their dedication to learning and their ability to recognize fundamental issues, as well as, perhaps, to their stiff-neckedness. They cared deeply about education. Because of their zeal they sometimes violently opposed the educational efforts of those with whom they disagreed; without that zeal, education would have developed much more slowly in many areas. Not all Presbyterians were so violently sectarian, or even Calvinistic, in their attitude toward human nature as the more bitter opponents of Cooper and Holley. Indeed, one of their most distinguished ministers, Philip Lindsley, took the lead in trying to establish in Tennessee a university dedicated to serving the entire community without becoming a tool of any particular group.

Lindsley came to Tennessee after beginning a most promising career in New Jersey. His distinction as a minister, and as a professor at Princeton, twice led the trustees of Transylvania to invite him to become president of the College. In 1817 he was elected vice president of Princeton; he served as its acting president in 1822, and in the next year was offered the presidency. Dickinson College and the new Ohio University at Athens also negotiated with him concerning the leadership of those institutions. One wonders why he chose in 1824 to become president of little Cumberland College in Nashville, Tennessee.

In 1806 Congress had granted the State of Tennessee 100,000 acres of land for the establishment of two universities. Blount College in East Tennessee and Cumberland College in Nashville, both Presbyterian colleges, became quasi-state universities in due time. Blount was ultimately to become the present University of Tennessee; Cumberland, by a long and tortuous journey (worthy of being retraced by those interested in the intricate interplay of sectarian, federal, state, and philanthropic support of education) ultimately became, in part, the George Peabody College for Teachers.

Though remaining in the hands of self-perpetuating boards, and seldom aided significantly by the state, these two institutions were viewed as representing the general interest in education. In 1809 the legislature passed an act providing that, "No ordinance, rule, or by-law should ever be entered into so as to give a preference to any one denomination of Christians," a statement which could be interpreted as tending toward secularism, at least insofar as it outlawed a rigorously dogmatic approach to truth.

After the reorganization of Cumberland as the University of Nashville in 1824, a sustained and reasonably successful attempt was made by Philip Lindsley to broaden the curriculum and raise standards to those appropriate to a university. Lindsley was not a thoroughgoing secularist. He was a Presbyterian whose Puritan bias clearly showed. "Show me," he said, "a poor man, in the enjoyment of his health, who never seeks to improve his position, and I will show you a man fit or fitting for the penitentiary or the gallows."[34] Nevertheless, he was scornful of colleges that pretended to be nonsectarian but which actually sought to proselyte students. This, he maintained, had never happened at Nashville. Carefully avoiding sectarian issues, he appealed to the common convictions of Christianity.[35] Like Horace Mann, and most Protestant leaders of his time, he saw no irony in the argument that freedom of religion and thought is assured as long as indoctrination is restricted to the common elements of Christianity, which became in fact the common elements of Protestantism.

Nor was he an advocate of highly utilitarian education. He worked hard to establish a multipurpose university with a wide range of professional schools and with the shops and experimental farms needed to provide training in the agricultural and mechanical arts; but he insisted that all higher education be centered on the liberal arts required of all educated people, and he constantly complained because his patrons were ever concerned about the vocational value of college training.

Lindsley clearly realized that the proliferation of small colleges and the fragmentation of educational support threatened to make adequate higher education impossible for all. He chose Nashville because it lay in the center of a vast and growing region where there were no competing colleges. The circle of its potential influence had a radius of 200 miles. If this potentially vast community could be rallied to the support of a single nonsectarian university, a great institution of higher education was achievable. Lindsley believed the necessary support would be forthcoming. "I did once flatter myself," he recalled in 1848, "that the people of Tennessee would rally around this infant seat of science, and take just pride in its growth and prosperity. I did suppose that they would cherish an institution of their own—established in their own flourishing metropolis—in the midst of their own territory, and of their peculiar manners, customs, climate, habits, and all those other nameless indescribable somethings which constitute *home*. . . . I did suppose that the good sense of the community would soon perceive that a university cannot be in every town—that it must have some one permanent location—and that, when once fixed and in operation, all petty jealousies and rivalries would die away."[36]

With characteristic missionary zeal Lindsley stumped the state of Tennessee, spreading the gospel of higher education. He noted that the new kind of higher education that combined liberal education with vocational and professional training gave all young people the opportunity for social mobility and promised to become the great balance wheel in the social and economic class struggle. He argued that moral instruction in the common elements of the Christian faith would mitigate the viciousness of sectarian conflict.

And the University of Nashville did rise to a position of distinction among American universities; but Lindsley failed. Within a decade Nashville's sphere of influence began to fill with denominational colleges. When he resigned in 1848 the once virgin ground was hostess to thirty institutions of higher education. Two years after his resignation the University was bankrupt and suspended operations. Despite heroic efforts he had been unable to defend the University against charges of "godlessness" and infidelity, or the city of Nashville against back-country charges of iniquity and aristocracy.

In 1854 the University was reorganized around a strong medical faculty, and after the Civil War a federally subsidized state normal school took over the facilities of the literary department. On this school was George Peabody College built.

The actions of Thomas Cooper, Horace Holley, and Philip Lindsley showed traces of the colors we identify with the modern state university. Signs of the day to come shone most brilliantly from Columbia, South Carolina, and were violently repressed. Though the trustees who manned the lights were elected officials and the legislators who controlled the public purse paid for the electricity, the switch was pulled when a harsh secular beam played too brightly into the recesses of sectarianism.

One would have thought the sun itself had risen over Lexington, but in a brief moment darkness again descended. A less brilliant, but more steady, glow hovered on the horizon at Nashville, but this too was a false dawn. Had we examined the sky over Virginia, and later over Michigan, we could, of course, have seen the new day come more steadily. But who, in a real dawn, looks only to the east and ignores the subtle play of black and white and red in the southern and western skies?

•

CHAPTER TWO

Pedagogical Polemics

and Politics

•

As far as possible, I would prepare every human being for that most important of all duties, the determining of his religious belief for himself.

HORACE MANN

[People] are just what surrounding circumstances make them; surrounding circumstances are under the control of church and state; ergo, it is church and state that make man the vicious, unhappy being we find him.

WILLIAM MACLURE

The first thing we need to do is to abate some of our stupid reverence for the law as it is, *and begin really to inquire after the law as it* ought to be.

JONATHAN BALDWIN TURNER

In its amplitude, zeal, and commitment to Man's progress the reform impulse of the pre-Civil War decades stands unmatched in American experience. Reformers fought for the abolition of slavery, for temperance, for greater religious tolerance in secular affairs; they inveighed against archaic penal practices, sought an end to war, argued for radical changes in dominant political and economic ideologies, and pressed for women's rights. An uncertain, if not skeptical, modern age looks with a blend of awe, nostalgia, and disbelief upon the efforts of those many persons who believed that reform was mankind's greatest calling. As Horace Greeley expressed this widely shared mood,

> not to have been a Reformer is not to have truly lived. Life is a bubble which any breath may dissolve; Wealth or Power a snow-flake, melting momently into the treacherous deep across whose waves we are floated on to our unseen destiny; but to have lived so that one less orphan is called to choose between starvation and infamy—one less slave feels the lash applied in mere wantonness and cruelty—to have lived so that some eyes of those whom Fame shall never know are brightened . . .—this surely is to have really *lived*—and not wholly in vain.[1]

No institution, no idea, was sacrosanct. Those who worked to re-form society so that Man might live in natural harmony with fellow man and with Nature grubbed at the weeds of injustice wherever they appeared. Emerson accurately reported that "Christianity, the laws, commerce, schools, the farm, the laboratory; and not a kingdom, town, statute, rite, calling, man, or woman, but is threatened by the new spirit."[2]

Radical many reformers were; but they were also nonviolent. They wrestled against the status quo with firmness but with a tender, if zealous, concern for touching all persons with the blessings of reform. So it was that many reformers pleaded a special case for education. They contended that education stood central to all reform activity. If the several humanitarian crusades were to bring lasting improvements, reformers argued, the ideal of meliorism would have to be sustained somehow from generation to generation. Universal free schools would cement the generations together in their common purposes. Wide support came for the idea that schooling for all youth posed a sound answer to disturbing questions about the enduring value of reform agitation. Education would elevate character. Economic efficiency would thereby increase and civic competence be heightened. By teaching the common elements of learning in public schools all across the land Americans would find that supreme respect had at last been paid to the idea of the dignity of Man. Ignorance had theretofore produced indolence, class privilege, and other hated hosts of evil against which reformers solidly set themselves. Learning would bring greater power as well as virtue to all whom it reached. It would supplant ignorance. Above all else, it would institutionalize the spirit of reform, the very mystique of Progress.

The crusade for education needed, and won, support from a vast coalition of interest groups. Humanitarianism alone did not account for the rise of common schools and, later, of land grant colleges in America. Many entrenched commercial and propertied interests, many Neo-Federalists, often supported educational reform while they criticized melioristic agitation in general. The noted politician Daniel Webster, for example, won no reputation as a reformer. Yet Webster, that "jackal of the vested interests," as Brooks Adams grumpily preferred to describe him, supported the common school movement.[3] He believed education would curb the impulsive restlessness of Man the Reformer. Webster sounded the alarum for the conservatives. Fear, not ardent optimism about man's nature, moved him. How long would social stability survive the inundation of European migrants, the civil disobedience and assertive individualism of many native-born, without the restraining power of education? A shared fear of man in the mass gave conservatives ample cause to appreciate Webster's praise of education as wise "system of police."[4]

Thus the arguments for free public education took many forms in the generation before the Civil War. Through ingenious application of the art of conciliation, reformers organized powerful coalitions of pro-education forces out of the several special interest groups. Educational reformers appealed, for example, to the employers' desire to have alert and obedient workers who were capable of following instructions and increasing production more than enough to offset the cost of educating them. Short-range private interests were encouraged by such appeals. Reformers also held out promises of social uplift through education and pleaded a case for learning as patient amelioration to these persons of the longer view. And the potential threat of battles among the many interest groups over control of the revitalized school systems was turned aside oratorically from the outset through repeated assurances that the school would stand above all class and ideological strife. Clearly the proposed public enterprise was to be thoroughly nonpartisan, serving all alike.

But friends of schooling widely disagreed about the nature and thrust of education and the community ideals it should advance. We turn now to examine the views of spokesmen for three competing notions of education and community: first, Horace Mann, who searched for common bonds by which to unite and guide beleaguered communities that no longer enjoyed simple tribal homogeneity; second, William Maclure, who despaired of community reform except through boarding schools which in effect permitted the good society to be built within, but not as a part of, the general community; and third, Jonathan Baldwin Turner, who held greatest hope for community reformation through a state-supported secular system of "useful" higher education, and who promoted the reformed university as the courtier of the modern state and as the agent charged to shift community leadership throughout the state from classically prepared elites to thoroughly tutored "industrious classes."

I

HORACE MANN: UNCOMPROMISING CONCILIATOR

The spectacular and tireless efforts of Horace Mann of Massachusetts showed the educational reformer at his agile best, sparring with clergymen, politicians, yeomen, and social gadflies. In speech, pamphlet, journal, and newspaper Mann turned objections into justifications for education. He played artfully upon the minds —and hearts—of those who feared (as he did) the extravagant evils of ignorance and mob behavior in the Jacksonian era. To those who preferred to trust to "common sense" he stressed formal learning as its prerequisite. Employees and employers, "consumers" and "producers," learned they both would profit from education. And when addressing friendly, already committed audiences, Mann provided inspirational sermons on education in general, calculated to sustain support already won. His mission as he saw it was to overcome apathy, soften suspicion, and win commitments to tax-supported public instruction. To be sure, he found pockets of outright opposition. But apathy and easy verbal agreement were his greatest enemies. One had to be overcome, the other mobilized in his support. While giving public orations on educational reform Mann worried little about being heckled from the crowd. He worried about losing his audiences outright to competing puppet- and monkey-shows, military bands, and hurdy-gurdies.[5] For his message was familiar, his theme widely understood. His successes against these diversionary obstacles came from the new sense of urgency and eloquent zeal he brought into the arena. Behind the scenes, moreover, he adroitly used his office and personal prestige to secure support from influential individuals; he worked through various action groups and organizations; and he used the presses to send his messages beyond the range of his voice. Through appeals to conscience, logic, and concern for America's mission, Mann thus worked to strengthen state and local statutory support for free schools throughout Massachusetts. From there his influence spread across the land.

Mann rightly judged that he would encounter men "who are accessible only through a single motive, or who are incased in prejudice and jealousy, and need, not to be subdued but to be remodelled! how many who will vociferate their devotion to the public, but whose thoughts will be intent upon themselves!" Mann had no illusions about winning easy support from those who themselves were well educated. "Many of our educated men need educating much more than the ignorant." So he steeled himself for formidable opposition on all fronts, believing that the learned and the ignorant alike had yet to be raised "to the level of humanity."[6]

In 1837, when Mann accepted the offer to become the first secretary of the Massachusetts Board of Education, he found it a modest office but a supreme challenge offering almost unlimited possibilities for a reformer. Trained in law, tested in politics, Mann understood the art of molding formless sentiment into formal legislation. And for what better cause than education could he apply his art? His *modus operandi* was to create an image of one possessed by "the spirit of self-abandonment, the spirit of martyrdom." This approach would lift him free from narrow partisanship; and before this image of statesmanlike martyrdom Mann believed

> there are but few, of all those who wear the form of humanity, who will not yield. I must not irritate, I must not humble, I must not degrade anyone in his own eyes. I must not present myself as a solid body to oppose an iron barrier to any. I must be a fluid sort of man, adapting myself to tastes, opinions, habits, manners, so far as this can be done without hypocrisy or insincerity, or a compromise of principle. In all this there must be a higher object than to win personal esteem, or favor, or worldly applause. A new fountain may now be opened. [He hoped to direct the flow of that fountain] in such a manner, that if, when I have departed from life, I may still be permitted to witness its course, I may behold it broadening and deepening in an everlasting progression of virtue and happiness.[7]

One might suspect that Mann could not have decided upon a more dubious and difficult course. His temperament was most ill suited to his idea of conquest through conciliation of the sort he described. In an important sense he nonetheless believed that he should become the personal embodiment of the common school ideal. Men should be able to see in his behavior and find reflected in his rhetoric the methodology and curriculum of ideal education for American life. But Mann the Unitarian fought with only moderate success against his Calvinistic upbringing. His commitment to fixed principle tended to remain uncompromisingly fierce. Behind his gold-bow spectacles his mind had sorted Right from Wrong and insisted that behavior follow accordingly. Erect in his long-tailed black coat he set himself with high indignation against every detected failure to follow Right and combat Wrong. No one remained uncertain as to Mann's attitude toward liquor, for example. On the question of slavery, his support of abolition was articulate and ardent. It was once said that had Mann been free of educational preoccupations during the 1840's "the Civil War might have started a decade sooner. . . ."[8]

Mann found it difficult to temper justice with mercy even among close acquaintances. His brother-in-law, the noted author Nathaniel Hawthorne, once inadvertently tested Mann's opposition to tobacco by mentioning that he enjoyed an occasional indulgence in cigars. Mann bristled. "Do I understand you to say, Mr. Hawthorne, that you actually use tobacco?" Hawthorne, left with the alternatives of claiming he had lied or testifying a second time to his use of tobacco, chose the honest course. His own composure unruffled, Hawthorne now watched bemused as Mann did battle with his conscience, pitting his affection for Hawthorne against his duty to uphold Right. Right won. Placing himself "tall and tragic" before Hawthorne, Mann "spoke in a husky voice to this effect: 'Then, Mr. Hawthorne, it is my duty to tell you that I no longer have the same respect for you that I have had.'"[9] With that, Mann strode from the room in silence.

Handling educational problems in a conciliatory manner, however, seemed to be a different matter to Mann. In the first place, since systematic public education had to be borne by the consent—and dollars—of diverse interest groups, Mann took great pains to demonstrate that the schools would stand apart from all special interests. There would be no favoritism in the schools; no house would be set against another by public education. On the contrary, the school would serve as the one nationwide "rallying-point for a peaceful and harmonious co-operation and fellowship, where all the good may join in the most beneficent of labors."[10] Believing that "The young do not come into life barbed and fanged against each other, . . ." Mann argued that education could therefore be expected to soften gradually the "alienating competitions of life" in America.[11] Had Mann not denied that education would be "curative and remedial," designed to "heal diseases and wounds," he might more freely have cast conciliatory restraints aside, as he did in combatting intemperance, slavery, and tobacco. But one who did battle with ignorance had to do so in the spirit of the ideal institution designed to end ignorance. The school came not to cure or remedy current ills, Mann declared. It came as a "preventive and an antidote" against their later occurence. Nor was it designed to heal social wounds so much as "to make the physical and moral frame invulnerable to them."[12] In time, then, a school conceived to "train up children in the elements of all good knowledge and of virtue" would make "nine-tenths of the crimes in the penal code" obsolete; "the long catalog of human ills would be abridged; men would walk more safely by day; every pillow would be more inviolable by night; property, life, and character would be held by a stronger tenure; all rational hopes *respecting the future* brightened."[13]

Clearly educational reform ought to be understood as distinct in kind and purpose from all other reform activity. There is little reason to doubt Mann's sincerity about preventing teachers from drawing student attention to divisive questions of the day, although, as Mann also admitted, such a policy made for sound political sense in educational statesmanship. "The moment it is known or supposed that the cause is to be perverted to, or connected with, any of the exciting party questions of the day, I shall never get another cent [for the common school campaign] I shall be bereft of all power in regard to individuals, if not in regard to the State."[14] Rather than risk any partisanship charges whatsoever, Mann elected to bar all contemporary issues from the classroom. His agitation for common school reform, even modestly restricted by such sensitivity, managed to elicit serious charges that Mann pleaded the case of special interests. Still, his self-designated task was to prove that there existed certain fundamental ideas shared by all Americans in senses educational, political, religious, and economic.

A second suggestive explanation for Mann's willingness to be conciliatory hinged upon his notion of those fundamental and shared American ideas. In every important sense his cluster of ideals suitable for the public school seemed to reflect his own personal credo. Politically, Mann hoped to see America become increasingly committed to "republicanism"—as opposed to Jacksonianism on the one hand and Neo-Federalism on the other— and Mann, a Whig himself, undoubtedly considered the common elements of American political ideology in harmony with the ideals of his party. Religiously, America hopefully was destined to espouse a "natural" faith system and grow beyond the unreasonable vagaries of "revealed" religion; and Mann, a Unitarian by persuasion, assuredly found the common elements of American religious faith mirrored in his own creed. Economically, American destiny called for a union between public charity and private enterprise; and Mann, an advocate of both *laissez-faire* and the doctrine of stewardship, once again felt his own commitments and the prophetic heart of American experience beating in unison. Mann's notion of the "common elements" suitable to the unique reform mission of the "common schools" took shape under the influence of his personal ideals. These generally stated ideals therefore did not appear likely to produce contentiousness. Let them be simply stated without belabored comment or explanation. In a naively optimistic age, a time filled with boundless faith in the power of education, Mann believed that the straightforward presentation of incontrovertible fact and moral principle would serve these ends ably. If teachers passed without comment over other material of controversial nature, then education would bring, of its own weight, right reason to all.

Mann's personal credo was forged largely out of his impassioned attempts to beat down the Calvinistic attitudes that dominated his youth. He worked diligently to find flaws in the doctrine of human depravity and the view of God as a Being of wrath and justice. His religious odyssey toward Unitarianism also led him toward full acceptance of human perfectibility, the potential goodness of man, and meliorism as the reasonable justification for bringing greater opportunity to the members of the human community. He recoiled from the dogmatic certainty with which Puritans and all other sectarians settled speculative issues. He came to have "the deepest aversion to sectarianism, and to all systems of proselytism among Christian sects."[15] They scattered discord; they did not bring light. "As far as possible," Mann therefore concluded, "I would prepare every human being for that most important of all duties, the determining of his religious belief for himself."[16] To teach a child only those elements of religion to which all sects subscribed seemed most true to the spirit of public school conciliation; it also faithfully represented Mann's own guiding purposes. "It seems to me that a generation so trained would have an infinitely better chance of getting at the truth than the present generation has had. I always look upon my own conclusions on questions of faith with a measure of distrust, lest I may have landed in possible error on one side, from the vigor of the spring which I gave to escape from what seemed certain error on the other."[17]

As Mann tugged against the restraints of Calvinism, what lasting marks did the exertion leave on his mind? Obviously he did not wrench completely free of his heritage. Nor did he try. On the contrary, he often merely secularized and thereby retained certain Puritan ideals that seemed to cut across all denominational lines, that revealed basic human impulses and needs. A sense of community, supported by all institutions and agencies, represented one such ideal. A good society would, in Mann's view, maintain homogeneity of values in matters of basic religious commitment, political ideology, and economic conviction. In like manner the model Puritan had also voiced his high approval of "calling" and "stewardship." Such ideals were worthy of universal adoption and perpetuation. In essential respects true to his Puritan heritage Mann labored with anxious zeal to rebuild a similar American concept of community solidarity and fundamental homogeneity. Such a sense of community had somehow to take new root in the United States. But it certainly would not serve to establish puritanism or any other recognizable orthodoxy across the land if this community ideal were to be nurtured in the public day schools. It was the nature of orthodoxies to impose their dogmas upon every individual and agency. Just so had the Puritans pressed church and school, hymnal and hornbook, business codes and blue laws into the service of their faith. The New Community would be far more tolerant of diversity of belief and conduct, for its residents would realize that an essential accord, a shared commitment to fundamental values, bound them each to each. As yet one more testament to the exuberant optimism of an age in education, Mann found much support for his idea that community life could be perfected through the single institution of common day school education. The school would be the repository of community ideals. It would perpetually remind men that wherein they differed was of vastly less significance than their united acceptance of basic principles. A school that fostered this sense of community, Mann believed, could find sanction and support as a secular ideal shared by Americans of diverse religious faiths, backgrounds, and aspirations. Someday it would become universally apparent that the schools were "the way that God has chosen for the reformation of the world."[18] They most certainly held the key to American destiny. Of education, alone among all objects of reform agitation, could it be said that no claim sounded too extravagant. "This institution is the greatest discovery ever made by man: we repeat it, *the common school is the greatest discovery ever made by man*."[19] Clearly Mann held education in the same esteem as had his Puritan forebears who candidly staked the future of their colonial venture upon the success of their education programs.

On the question of human depravity, Horace Mann did not completely repudiate the Puritan assertion that the child's original evil inclinations made proper education doubly imperative. Thus, although he came to accept the doctrines of progress and human perfectibility, he also carried into his mature years the belief that every child came into life with "latent capabilities of evil." Unrestrained, these capabilities or "propensities" unleashed the effects of human depravity. Properly restrained, man's evil propensities could be governed, but not destroyed. Control, restrain, govern them, yes; but annihilate them? Probably not. Nature, Mann asserted in one mood, "reproduces them with every human being that comes into the world."[20]

How does one perform the mental gymnastics necessary to link faith in human progress to the doctrine of human depravity? Mann formed the union by adding two conceptual braces. First, he noted that man possessed noble propensities as well as ignoble. To believe that Providence endowed mankind with "terrible propensities" alone, Mann called "impious."[21] Rather, the Creator not only added noble propensities, He made it possible for them to become the dominant and controlling ones. Properly educated, every child could learn to exercise reason and thus respond to his conscience. He thereby would learn to follow his innate noble propensities and to ignore the dictates of passion and appetite through which innate evil would dominate him entirely. If men were to be saved from servitude to innate evil, however, they had to be educated, and well, while children. Mann wrote that the task of overcoming evil with the good in man *"must be mainly done during the docile and teachable years of childhood."*[22]

Second, his acceptance of phrenology as a true science of the human mind enabled him to argue that man's evil propensities might be severely stunted, perhaps someday even prohibited from influencing human behavior. Mann believed the brain to be the repository of all human propensities (or, more appropriately in this context, "faculties"). These faculties, humane and atavistic alike, had been identified and analyzed by phrenologists, notably by Horace Mann's close friend, the internationally famous George Combe from England. The new science of mind had further assigned to discrete segments of the hemispheres of the brain each of man's known faculties. The mechanistic attitude nurtured carefully by many Lockean and Newtonian followers, Mann included, further encouraged phrenological assertions that mind could best be understood as a network of muscles. Each faculty was a muscle. A trained eye and a sensitive hand, some even contended, could discern the strength of many muscular faculties by studying cranial formations. A child's head, with its peculiar irregularities from forehead to tip of spinal column, became for Mann the equivalent of twentieth century "objective tests" of aptitude and ability. Depressions and bulges in the head indicated which faculties were exceedingly weak and strong, respectively. The day of a science of learning seemed to have dawned. Phrenology stood as the new Queen of Sciences. Now a properly trained teacher could determine which of a child's faculties need special exercise and which should be left unemployed, either to atrophy into helplessness or return to a more normal balance of strength with other faculties.

Phrenology offered Mann confident assurance that evil propensities or faculties could be withered and the nobler ones "exercised." Phrenology further enabled Mann to make peace between his ingrained suspicions about depravity and his hope for human progress through amelioration. In this instance as well as others Mann was thus temperamentally conservative and intellectually liberal in his response to an enduring question about human nature. When he addressed conservative groups he knew and shared their fears for America's future if it were left in the hands of the uneducated. He engaged in no duplicity when he warned them of the evil nature of man when left unrestrained by learning. Addressing audiences dominated by optimism about man's nature he could prophesy human progress through universal education with personal commitment ringing in every phrase. The Janus symbol depicted human nature for him; and political acumen helped him decide which face to describe to a given audience.

Mann was certainly no radical reformer. With the outstanding exception of the "peculiar institution" of human slavery, he left untouched the basic framework of American institutional practices. He preached education as ecumenicism from long years of associating with Americans who pondered the problems and promises of *e pluribus unum*, out of many, one. He was a fighter, but no fighting liberal. He more often viewed the school as an agency of social control than, for example, as an establishment to promote individual freedom of thought and speech. If he spoke of such freedoms as ends he did not consider them as necessary pedagogical means. He freely chose to exclude discussions of controversial subjects from the classroom, without seriously entertaining the warning that free and deliberative exchanges of views were the bulwarks against the spread of propagandistic doctrines among an inert people. By no means swept up by Jacksonianism he aligned himself with the politically negative elements of Whiggery. He lent weight in fact to certain strains of political Know-Nothingism by asserting that the common school should advance the cause of Protestant Christianity alone.[23] No other theistic or nontheistic belief could support the common purposes of public education.

It borders on the ironic that Mann, commonly remembered as a liberal, can as readily be understood as one who labored to establish an essentially socialistic institution, public education in the interests of enlightened conservatism. His strength as an educational reformer rested with his tenacity, his firmness of character, his admirable rhetorical skills, and his political acumen, all of which enabled him to turn political, economic, and religious centers of power to his "nonpartisan" educational purposes. At the same time there was in him that peculiar ambivalence that produced an intense dedication to humanitarianism. It propelled him, as did his belief that man's predicament could be dramatically alleviated by human reason alone; that all Americans, regardless of race or disparity of opinions on a wide variety of speculative subjects, should and could be drawn into full membership in the community; and that common allegiance to generally stated fundamentals of American life did not call for the imposition of thoroughgoing homogeneity upon a free people. He was at home among all agitators so inclined. Two months before he died in August 1859, he restated an injunction that had for years driven him from cause to cause: "Be ashamed to die until you have won some victory for humanity."[24] For him, to have contributed so effectively to the common school revival must have constituted one such victory.

WILLIAM MACLURE: EDUCATIONAL FREETHOUGHT ON THE FRONTIER

A modern age anxious about the school's present and historical encouragement of creative intelligence will find only modest support from the Horace Manns, the Henry Barnards, the Caleb Millses, and other shapers of state systems of public instruction in antebellum America. Their task was primarily one of converting lip service to education into three-dimensional reality. Still, it is a truth of small comfort that to search for strong strands of support for institutionalized "free inquiry" in nineteenth-century America is to reap meager rewards for arduous toil. The firm but gentle rigor of humane scholarship and an attendant tolerant spirit of reason did not then rule. Some observers despair that America will ever be adequately congenial to the reformer who seeks the necessary popular support and recognition of the importance of creative intelligence. Proponents of the development of critical thought in public schools can, with devastatingly effective ease, document the charges that Horace Mann and many other leading educational reformers were largely preoccupied with vocational, civic, and moral considerations; that they were too unconcerned or too rhapsodically enamored of childlife; and that they embarrassed later generations with their penchants for Protestantism inviolate. They did commendably transform an amazingly strong faith in something called "education" into a public institution without parallel in the modern world. But their customary attitude toward the higher promises of "free inquiry" and formal-and-informal learning remained suspicious, and, as the cases of Horace Holley, Phillip Lindsley, and Thomas Cooper bore witness, at times hostile.

But much prophetic private experimentation and public agitation was conducted in support of the temporarily lost causes of these college presidents. Other minority reports claimed wider horizons for man and society. Thoreau found some of his deepest gratifications as the schoolmaster of his unorthodox and "uncommon" school. Emerson at least talked about a Rousseauian education based upon child interest and spontaneity as best serving the mental independence of "man thinking." The historian George Bancroft and the entrepreneur Robert Owen and others of similar repute organized private schools dedicated to excellence as they understood the application of such a term to "education." Experiment and dissent continued apace. One such fighting dissenter, William Maclure, illustrated elements of a more thoroughgoing dedication to secular learning for American youth to whom far greater credit for creative intelligence had been assigned.

The efforts of William Maclure (1763-1840) as a radical educational reformer were but one in a series of noteworthy achievements for which the undeservedly obscure Maclure should receive credit. In the last decades of the eighteenth century this ambitious Scotsman served as a partner in a London merchant firm, an enterprise that took him back and forth between England and the United States. So profitable were his business affairs and so convinced was he that with America rode the best possibilities for improving the lot of mankind, that he came to the United States to "retire" in 1803 at the age of forty.[25]

His retirement was at least as strenuous and easily more productive and exciting than his years in business. With a keen and scholarly interest in science—especially geology—Maclure set out in 1807 upon a one-man tour of almost every state and territory in the nation, gathering research data for the first geological survey of the United States. In 1809 and again in 1818 he submitted maps and reports of his epoch-making survey to the American Philosophical Society in Philadelphia. A member of the Society since 1799, he served on its council from 1818 to 1829. In 1812 he joined the Academy of Natural Sciences. Seven years later, and continuing thereafter until his death in 1840, Maclure served as the president of the academy, a tenure of nearly twenty-two years. His original national survey having won him recognition as America's foremost geologist, he became the first president of the American Geological Society in 1819. Maclure also had served in France as a member of the American Spoliation Commission, established by the Jefferson administration in 1803 to settle American claims against the French government.

It was while serving on this commission that Maclure visited and became tremendously excited about the educational reform activities of Johann Pestalozzi's schools then arousing much interest in Europe. Maclure became the first important Pestalozzian in the United States. Thus over the years as Maclure established his reputation as a scientist, philanthropist, and friend of universal education, the broad outlines of a blueprint for human happiness began to form in his mind. Education became for him the key to a Good Society for man.

By 1825 Maclure's radical social philosophy had reached full formulation. And in that year he joined forces with the famous Welch entrepreneur and social reformer Robert Owen in a widely publicized experiment in social planning at New Harmony, Indiana. Early high hopes for the educational program at New Harmony abounded. With Maclure's prestige and infectious enthusiasm attracting famous scientists and educators to New Harmony, with Maclure enlisting such Pestalozzian specialists as Joseph Neef, Marie Duclos Fretageot, and Philip d'Arusmont and ordering a "vast collection" of books and scientific instruments to be shipped from New Orleans, New Harmony seemed to be building "the best Library and the best School in the United States."[26]

Operating from this base, as titular schoolmaster, Maclure described an educational program deemed suitable for a free people. Unlike Mann, whose conceptions of an ideal school sprang from the hope that fundamentally all men could be made to compete more humanely through the influence of day schools, Maclure argued for the resurrection of the humanistic boarding school to combat the vulgarities and confusions of contemporary community life. Maclure further wholeheartedly accepted the Jacksonian conception of class conflict. His world was one in which the laborers, the "producers" of wealth, struggled against the aristocratic clique, the "consumers" of wealth.

The principle theme of Maclure's social philosophy was that power and property in society could be balanced and made consonant with nature's laws only through equal educational opportunity for all. He held social and political equality to be the only conditions under which man could become a truly human moral creature. But clearly Western man had only begun to accept morality on its own unequivocal terms. Noting that nations were rich, while the millions were poor, that the church taught Christian brotherhood while practicing deception and theft; that governments hailed laissez-faire and set up monopolies; and that church and state declared their faith in brotherhood and social harmony, but colluded to forge antagonisms and discord, Maclure asked;

Whence comes all those contradictions, all those causes of mischief and misery? From the ignorance of the producers, who permit their representatives to expend the money of their constituents, in colleges and universities, for the instruction of their own children, and little or none for free schools for the education of the children of the laborer, who produces all. This is the true original sin, which descends from father to son and pollutes generations yet unborn.[27]

It was consistent with this view that Maclure refused to respond to pleas for his financial support of a proposed national
university at Washington. Such a university, in his judgment, would
only increase the inequality in the distribution of knowledge; and
it was already at a dangerous peak. Rather, he countered, let such
collected funds first be used in advancing the cause of popular
education. In America he believed he could see minds and conditions fresh enough to understand that morality—the fruit of popular education and general equality—represented the truly virtuous
result of the enlightened acceptance of "the selfish principle, which
rules and governs our species."[28]

In implicit agreement with enlightenment views as shared even
by Helvetius and Rousseau, Maclure believed that "self-interest"
not only was in fact the driving force in human behavior, but that
it need not be socially malevolent. Selfishness was evil; enlightened
self-interest was good. Operating as they must upon the "selfish
principle," the educated few were therefore acutely aware that
their power over the many depended upon widespread ignorance.
Hint to a man in power that you believe knowledge can be dis-
seminated to the many and at no great cost, Maclure argued, "and
you alarm him, by advocating a plan that would deprive him of the
greatest part of his power; and acting upon his own interest (and
it would be foolish to expect otherwise) he cannot do otherwise
than oppose your reform with all his might."[29] Maclure never tired
of repeating the Baconian reminder: Knowledge is power. Only
an equal distribution of knowledge would lead to a similar division
of power and property.

A great ideological gap separated Mann and Maclure. With
the concept of class struggle central in his writings, Maclure insisted that sound education could not proceed out of a day school
that hoped to mediate value conflicts in the community. For the
only value systems consulted would be those of the most powerful
(and willful) cliques in the community. Education could not serve
the interests of egalitarianism and teach a watered-down version
of aristocratic doctrines of elitism. To see the pedagogical problem
aright one had to acknowledge the existence of the great wall
separating producers and consumers. The struggle to bring educational opportunities to all American youth was also a struggle to
establish across the land a value system appropriate to the overwhelming numerical majority of Americans who were producers
of the nation's wealth. It was at the same time a struggle of the
"have-nots" against the "haves"; but basically it was a struggle of
the "ignorant" against the "educated."

Mann's denial of the rift between a deprived majority and a
willful minority would have been heresy enough to Maclure. Had

he lived long enough to trace Mann's advocacy of educational reform through day schools, however, Maclure would have denied
that Mann deserved any claim to be a reformer. Maclure agreed
fully with Robert Dale Owen, the eldest son of Robert Owen, who
declared that day schools "cannot regenerate a nation. . . . Let
those who desire common day schools speak out at once. They do
not desire the regeneration of this country."[30] But Maclure did
desire it. He promised to demonstrate how education could regenerate society and backed up his promise with his boarding school.
Those who shared his faith in the malleability of human nature
knew that through the boarding school Maclure might regularly
deliver results forever unattainable by a Horace Mann in a competing day school.

The boarding school kept the seamless robe of education in-
tact. Respect for learning and for the highest values in the community, carefully nurtured by the teacher, met none of the
discouraging setbacks common to the day school program. It
seemed inconceivable to Maclure that reformers could expect a
day school teacher, given but a few hours each week, to lift his
charges out of the crosscurrents of conflicting values which swirled
within the community. A swipe at literacy and a dash through some
calculations summed up the accomplishments of the day school;
it might raise standards of living but it left the quality of life untouched. Or, it was even possible that the day school actually spread
confusion and cynicism. It held aloft democratic values while it
regularly returned the child to the world of extreme opulence and
poverty, curses and drunkenness. It permitted the child to go home
each evening, with words of respect for learning still ringing in his
ears, to hear contradictory lectures from his lay elders on the ef-
feminacy of education, on the superiority of homespun wisdom,
on the philosophy of "get others before they get you," coarse
language, selfishness, and dollars. In whom, in what was the child
to believe? Believing that inadequate and destructive parents were
to be found at all levels of society, Maclure urged that the boarding
school be used to solve the vast problems of human inequities.

For all of Maclure's militant opposition to the "consumers"
(primarily clergymen and politicians) his educational program
bore the stamp of radicalism owing primarily to his insistence that
all public education be in boarding schools. Throughout the tradition of radical educational reform thought similar insistence has
been heard repeatedly. With such men as Plato, Jonathan Swift,
Claude Helvetius, and other humanistic reformers in the Western tradition, and with Joseph Neef, Robert Dale Owen, Frances
Wright, and several Shaker educators in America during his lifetime, Maclure also advocated the separation of the child from the

controlling power of his parents.[31] Children of the well-to-do, regularly before (and since) Maclure's time, had gone to such schools. The Etons and Rugbys, the private academies and prep schools in England and America, were to sustain this tradition. For Maclure, then, as for others who have linked education to a vision of a better tomorrow, "education" meant far more than formal learning. For them education was euthenics; the conscious control of all environmental factors in the interest of philosophical views that shape an ideal individual for an ideal state. More specifically, "education" was a twofold process: one formal, the other informal. As a formal process, it manifested itself in agencies designed to teach skills, disseminate information, and guide physical development. No less important, on the other hand, informal education described the responsibility of all other agencies to reinforce the moral, mental, physical, and aesthetic aims of formal education for a Good Society.

While Maclure's quest for a Good Society had been primarily a search for a sound format of formal education, it remained vital that informal education be restrained from working at cross-purposes with the school. Maclure believed (as did later Americans as divergent in many respects as G. Stanley Hall, B. F. Skinner, and others who have equated education with euthenics) that the supreme justification for the existence of the community was its role as an educational agency.[32] All other activities and institutions in a Good Society should be subsumed under the task of elevating and perfecting man as a social creature. Stated negatively, for such reformers the fundamental challenges to human progress were resistance to the advancement of knowledge and resistance to scientifically controlled social change. The home, no less than church and state, was seen as a powerful source of such resistance. With little hope for sudden macrocosmic change, Maclure insisted that gradual reform through the boarding school represented the surest means of elevating society.

In Maclure's plan for free boarding schools, children from all walks of life would share the experience of education in the realm of positive knowledge. Their meals would be nourishing and simple; their clothing designed for the comfort of active youth. Between 5:00 A.M. and 8:00 P.M., with three hours reserved for meals, and no more than one hour at each particular study, the children would be occupied profitably and without fatigue. They would learn to withhold judgment, to think critically, and to recognize and respect the power of knowledge as a lever for personal gratification and social reconstruction; they would gain respect for reason and enlightened self-interest. They would recognize the moral superiority of the American experiment in democracy, and they would realize that, as with other experiments, man has the right and responsibility to improve upon this one as new knowledge and richer insights come to him. Maclure hoped to see his boarding school plan spread from New Harmony across the nation, providing equal educational opportunities for all children at the public expense. This was an event "devoutly to be wished for," he wrote; "and when put into judicious practice, it will be one of the greatest and most beneficial revolutions that ever improved the destinies of mankind." Then would man's full mental force be bent into the service of happiness as "the end and object of all rational beings. . . ."[33]

Howls of protest greeted Maclure's (and later, Robert Dale Owen's) boarding school idea. Even parents who reserved tender loving care for livestock and left their children to their own devices resented the notion. The plan smacked of the "arrogant" belief that strangers could surpass parents in the raising of children. And of no little consequence, it meant that "someone else" would have to tend to the daily chores at home. For the entrepreneur who hoped to hire cheap and sell dear it threatened to pinch his supply of child laborers. But only those who understood the power of a controlled environment over the child's plastic nature grasped the ideological significance of this major point in Maclure's pedagogical creed.

Clergymen and political leaders provided the main stumbling blocks to universal boarding school education, according to Maclure. He hid little bitterness from his readers in describing the mockery preachers and politicians made of human affairs.

> There are two things which the ignorance and delusions of the great mass of mankind have never permitted their common sense to examine into, or pass judgment upon, though essential to their peace, comfort, and happiness. I mean politics and religion. . . . The few who move the wires and play the puppets behind the scenes, are alone informed of the legerdemain and phantasmagoria, which elude the blunted senses of the multitude.
> "The world is a farce, and all things show it;
> I thought so once, but now I know it."
> And the principal actors in this farce are politics and religion, personified by church and state. To this farce the people are admitted, those who labor the most, paying the dearest for a ticket of admission to this graduated theatre, where the expectants of office . . . are placed nearest the stage, having an interest in prospective, for concealing the mystery. Whilst the producing millions, whose labor main-

tains all, are pushed back into a dark corner, whence they can only perceive the various disguises assumed by the actors to dupe them out of their hard earned wages.[34]

In Maclure's eyes modern business practices had opened the floodgates to a rampaging acquisitiveness that had set man against man in a desperate struggle for wealth and power. The producers of wealth—the laboring classes—were denied the fruits of their labors, while church and state—whose members were nonproducers all—consumed the wealth of others. It seemed to Maclure that only the ignorance of the many permitted the few to enjoy this immoral monoply. He argued,

> The only thing belonging to the millions, that the unproductive few are interested in augmenting, is that part of their production which the few live upon; to increase which it has been generally conceived necessary to leave the productive class in ignorance, that they may be more peaceable, and better "hewers of wood and drawers of water."[35]

Inequality always follows in the wake of ignorance; and gross inequality is contrary to nature itself, he charged. "All the undisturbed operations of nature tend to equalize opportunity, both in the savage and civilized societies; for necessity, that spur to industry, leading to knowledge, is only to be found in the middle and lower ranks."[36] But man had indeed disturbed natural operations. He had not only permitted, he had also advocated an unequal distribution of knowledge. Maclure reasoned that largely from this, the concentration of knowledge in the hands of the few, had proceeded most of the evils of society in the Jacksonian era; it had permitted property and power to flow into those same hands. Thus "the free circulation of knowledge is opposed by a host of enemies, who by education and interest, are drilled to obstruct the dissemination of useful information." Hope for lasting equality, meanwhile, hinged upon the successful universalization of education, upon providing every child the opportunity to become a humane and moral creature. The producers therefore had to look to themselves for educational leadership. To expect help from the consumers "would be to expect an effect without a cause."[37]

Maclure assigned to environment the full responsibility for molding human behavior. While Horace Mann was to hit upon the notion that the child was born with a host of noble and ignoble faculties, Maclure hewed closer to the line drawn by Locke's *tabula rasa*. Society held the soft clay of human nature in its hand and by whim or design pressed it into final form. The world was too much with Maclure, however, for him to believe that an adult's nature remained malleable. The plasticity of human nature, accepted without question with respect to children, seemed to decrease at a discouraging rate for each person with each succeeding year of his life. Adults, therefore, could be described as those firmly bound by the institutions which nurtured them; in their formative years they had learned either the techniques for perpetuating those institutions to their own self-interest or to acquiesce in them as permanent, however oppressive. To operate effectively upon the principle of the plasticity of human nature, to make equality a permanent condition of American society, Maclure insisted, required patient work with youth. The process of equality, then, was slow, accelerating only in later years as the currently powerful enemies of equality gave place to new generations of youth educated to recognize their own self-interest and to respect the self-interest of others. "One thing seems proven by all our experiences," he noted, "that anything like a radical reform must be through the education of children."[38] On this point Mann and Maclure spoke with one voice. Maclure was clearly the more orthodox sensationalist in reasoning that all persons "are just what surrounding circumstances make them; surrounding circumstances are under the control of church and state; ergo, it is church and state that make man the vicious, ignorant, unhappy being we find him."[39] Innate evil and congenital good were macabre fantasies. Environment alone produced evil—and good.

Just as anything resembling a permanent establishment of equality depended heavily upon the successful division of knowledge among all the citizenry, so did the successful division of knowledge depend in turn upon Maclure's special version of Pestalozzian education, a version which Pestalozzi himself would likely have rejected. Too long had mankind been victimized by the "ancient, monkish system" of education whereby lofty abstractions and unquestioned cosmic assumptions served to divert men from studying the natural forces that bound them. Long overdue was the drive to release youthful curiosity from the deadly *ipse dixit* of traditional education. Maclure called it a supreme improvement in education to teach the pupil

> to derive his knowledge directly from the things themselves, or accurate representations of them. Instruct children to teach themselves by their own observations, which make lasting impressions, and enlist self-love to enhance the value of the knowledge acquired. This direct mode of instruction is entirely free from the delusions of the imagination, or local or individual prejudices, which warp, and too often hide in mystery the discourses of the professors.[40]

True to his faith in sense realism in education as the sole guide to lasting social reform, Maclure insisted that only after he had examined fifty alumni of the Pestalozzian system did he willingly accept its claim to superiority over the other systems. Also, at once true to his belief in self-interest as man's necessary and basic goad and to his belief in the revolutionary powers of Pestalozzian education, Maclure readily granted that "the Pestalozzian system ought to be feared and rejected by all despots and tyrants. . . ." As a logical counter-consequence of these same beliefs, Pestalozzian education "ought to be courted and encouraged by all those who possess and know the value of freedom; which proves the folly, stupidity, not to say crime, of free nations, copying or following the example of despots, tyrants, or monarchs, in any of their forms or practices . . . ." Maclure welcomed with alacrity all attacks which were directed against Pestalozzianism's failure to develop the power of imagination, to lift the pupil on poetic wings into the region of chimeras, or to open his ears to the music of the spheres; for these "shortcomings" were precisely the virtues of Pestalozzianism as interpreted by Maclure.[41] Facts, verifiable and empirical, and facts alone constituted the proper concern of the education program. Of such was the stuff of true knowledge which would bring to men greater equities of power and property.

The sheer excitement of coming to grips with reality and probing for the secrets of nature and social structures in the Pestalozzian manner also accelerated the progress of the pupil toward self-reliance and social competence. By teaching useful occupations Pestalozzianism also produced "both knowledge and property" and encouraged "habits of working and thinking conjointly, which last during life, and double the powers of production, while [alleviating] the fatigue of labor by a more agreeable occupation of the mind." Above all, the strict exclusion of all prejudices, opinions, "delusions of imagination," and dogmatisms would give dynamic life to a new freedom of inquiry and understanding of the world of the senses.[42] And because the sexes would be treated equally in the new educational program, "the mental force of the great mass of mankind" would be doubled from the outset.[43]

Maclure's program, like that of his ideal Pestalozzian teacher, Joseph Neef, developed around natural history with a pervasive reliance upon sense realism. Not only did natural history permit the development of simple ideas into complex constructs through the "direct use" of the senses, it also militated against ennui for the student. Pleased, amused (hopefully excited) with nature's endless variety, the student acquired a keen familiarity with reality. Above all, when properly led, he acquired the habit of diligent observation and examination and learned the wisdom of suspending judgment until an investigation had been completed.[44]

Maclure excluded rhetoric, declamation, and *belles lettres* from his curriculum, for these studies "only serve to disguise the truth and puzzle all who attempt to convert them into common sense." Mankind needed, first of all, a "plain simple narrative of facts."[45] Literature, which included these three suspect studies, could come only later, if at all—after correct facts and undistorted concepts of the natural world had been gained. Imagination is too much with us as it is, Maclure insisted. There are still those among us, he observed, who talk about innate ideas, for example, despite the fact that this notion has been "exploded." Indeed, he continued, some still pay homage to genius, talent, and wisdom as hereditary acquisitions and fail to account for the foolish children many wise men sire. Maclure begged men to remain in this world, cognizant of their potential power to shape environment, and urged them to build better homes for man on earth rather than erect uninhabitable castles in the air. All animals probably dream when asleep, "but our species is perhaps the only one that dreams when awake. . . ."[46]

Here was Neef's brand of sense realism applied with a vengeance. To those who would have begged that poetry be included as a desirable study, Maclure replied that poetry is applauded by those who cannot stand truth, and who spurn reality as beneath their dignity. On the other hand, Maclure had no objection to the fine arts—if they produced representations of reality; but let there be no gods, goddesses, myths, or portraits of tyrants created for the edification of the "consumers," that is, the nonproducers in society, the power-hungry clergymen and politicians.[47]

Clearly much more than the superiority of fact over fiction explained Maclure's narrow, relentless application of sense realism. His educational program embodied more than his materialism, his faith in universal education as the great leveling social force, and his determination to enable men to master their environment. It embodied even more than his rigorous preference for "useful" as opposed to "ornamental" studies. Behind the "old" education of the Latin Grammar School and classical studies in general, Maclure saw the doctrine of elitism, the sullen belief that the ignorance and inferiority of the mass of mankind could be demonstrated by its inability to pass successfully through the classical school. Maclure held high contempt for this doctrine. He believed it to have been conceived either in blindness or deception, and probably in both.

In truth, said Maclure, the mass of mankind finds the old curriculum impractical. For this reason they are seemingly unable to cut the traditional mustard, he added. But, left in ignorance as a consequence, they are taught to believe the myth of their own inferiority before the awesome splendor of a Latin-mouthing pastor or a Cicero-quoting politician. They are further taught what to think; and never would a nonproducer jeopardize his hegemony over the ignorant by informing them how to think for themselves. They are taught to turn their thoughts to the golden streets and ivory palaces in another world to come, while they dutifully build palaces and avenues for priests and kings in this world. This, Maclure charged, is the fruit borne of educating the few and indoctrinating the many with myths and visions so that they will suffer despotism patiently.[48]

Hence, no poetry, *belles lettres*, rhetoric, flights of fancy, or delusions regarding self-interest were to invade Maclure's school. Even the historian would have to send his printed wares elsewhere. Maclure charged the historians, past and present, with twisting the evils of tyranny, despotism, and church-state dominion into colorful pageants of great deeds performed by great men. Not until historians began to trace the common man's persistent, painful upward struggle toward freedom should history books find a market in the schools of Macluriana.[49]

If Maclure would permit the teaching of facts alone, how would he justify a program of indoctrination in the virtues of equality? For him, morality, not equality *per se*, would be taught. Equality need have no special attention drawn to it, because equality would describe the actual conditions of the school itself.

> Morality [he said] is easier taught in schools where nearly a perfect equality exists . . . . Equality in schools is as much more necessary and useful, than in adult societies, as the impressions are stronger and more lasting; and to remove any temptation to partiality, it might perhaps be well to exclude the children of masters or professors, from their own school, as much for their own good as for the benefit of the school.

Maclure's next sentence revealed that equality was not pure cooperation: "*Equality leaves fair scope for competition;* just and impartial decisions give a useful stimulus to exertion."[50]

Accepting for the moment Maclure's insistence that equality need not be taught directly, would he not have to indoctrinate his students to pass on to them his militant contempt for the practices of ambitious clergymen and politicians? Maclure, perhaps in anticipation of this query, and undoubtedly as a result of his advocacy of reason and consistency, replied in effect: Indeed church and state are the archenemies of equality. But because their power rests upon the enforced ignorance of the many as supplemented by emotional propaganda, the school need never attack them directly. The school's objective assault on general ignorance will serve this end.

It followed for Maclure that not only must the positive reliance upon facts be rigidly adhered to, but all opinions on speculative matters—religion and statecraft—must be excluded with equal sternness. Opinions on these matters constituted propaganda, regardless of how certain one might have been that they represented eternal verities. Moreover, the superiority of strict reliance upon positive knowledge could be demonstrated in another manner. In direct opposition to Horace Mann's search for "common elements" and ecumenism in matters religious and political, Maclure called these "opinions" and cast them out.

> If any preacher or teacher, would impartially examine how often he has changed his opinions on all speculative subjects, he must conclude, that he was in error before every change, and he was not only wrong himself, but led into error all that had confidence in his opinions . . . , [Maclure insisted]. An orthodox Christian, who had been preaching all his life-time that there were three Gods, and at the same time only one God, when he changes to a unitarian and proclaims only one God, must be convinced that he had, for half his life-time, preached error and falsehood, and propagated deception; and the like consequences must ensue, if the unitarian become a universalist; and the same on every change of opinion.[51]

Opinions, believed Maclure, are too changeable, too treacherous, to find their way into the teacher's conversations with pupils. As long as the "conclusions" remain on the level of faith or opinion, they do not constitute truth. "Positive knowledge of matter, motion, and mankind, is truth," while opinions invariably lack conclusive facts. "*It is therefore probable, that positively useful knowledge, conveyed through the medium of our sense, ought to be the chief object of all systems of education.*"[52] In short, Maclure made much of his observation:

> Nothing is more changeable or precarious than opinions. One who obtains possession of power, has not the same opinions, as when he was subjected to obey power. . . . When a man is sick, he thinks differently from a strong man; a young man from an old man . . . . and any and every man who acquires more correct information must change his opinions. . . . One may as reasonably quarrel with another

for having a nose longer or shorter, as for having an opinion different from his own.[53]

Clearly Maclure saw church and state in the perspective of history as propagators of opinions, opinions calculated to replace an education for reason and liberty with an indoctrination for subservience. Opinion, in this sense, blinded man to his own self-interest. Positive knowledge, conversely, awoke man to his own interests and provided him with the means whereby that interest might be satisfied in harmony with social interest. Therefore, "all free people ought to be on their guard against . . . flattery and adulation" from men in high places, warned Maclure.

> Substitute the word *my* for their word *public*, in all their declamatory orations, and change those of philanthropy, patriotism, benevolence, charity, etc., which issue from the pulpit or the forum, into *self-interest* as the only possible means of not being deceived, and made the dupes of religious or political quacks.[54]

Behind many noble schemes and polemics for universal education in the common schools, Maclure detected both the clear cry for social harmony, which he approved, and the deplorable absence of any awareness that the boarding school concept must be these reformers' initial consideration. Without the boarding school, teachers remained mere "hirelings," hence less than first-rate citizens. And although their pupils did gain fleeting glimpses of social harmony they returned to their homes only to become confused and hardened by parental ignorance and social contradiction in the community. This incessant exposure to value conflicts plus the picture of children sitting as self-styled prisoners on stools for a few hours and then racing toward the school exist and "freedom" at the end of each day, were repugnant to Maclure.[55]

Maclure did not expect the schools alone to carry the burden of social advance, however. He believed that the totality of his educational aims necessarily involved all friends of the program in a commitment to social justice in every avenue of life. Workers, especially, he encouraged to fight the battle of the ballots, pressing organized labor strength into the service of those candidates for public office who shared concern for equality in America; and Maclure pamphleteered with equal vigor for universal suffrage, state sovereignty, mechanics' institutes, libraries, and against banks, privilege, and inheritance—with steady respect for democratic processes and majority rule. A sustained attack upon ignorance and upon the unproductive few who thrived on the ignorance of the many became for Maclure a twofold mission in the name of equality. He wrote,

> Let us hope that a just equality will unite the whole human family in one common interest, taught by experience, that liberty without equality is but a name . . . ; that great inequality of property, knowledge and power must originate great abuses. . . .
>
> Let those who sneer and deride at such [hopes for the future] . . . as Utopian dreams, look at the progress of humanity for the last fifty years [c. 1780-1830], and tax their ingenuity for some sophistry to prove that it cannot continue in an accelerated motion; let those who by artifice and combination have usurped a temporary superiority over their fellow citizens, consider that their power is founded on the ignorance of those they control, which is every day dissipating by the various means and facilities of acquiring useful knowledge.[56]

Maclure's dedication to equality through education possessed him. When he was not penning an essay on the theme, he could probably have been found talking about it. While in New Orleans, for example, Maclure once met Frances Trollope. According to that witty and often acid-tongued commentator on life in Jacksonian America, she quickly wearied of Maclure, "who in the course of five minutes propounded as many axioms. . . ." Axioms or no, even she did not fully resist their impact. For while she carefully recorded her disdain of his "lofty imaginings of faultless systems," she neglected to add that those "lofty imaginings" had not prevented her from sending her son Henry to Maclure's school at New Harmony.[57]

Mrs. Trollope thought him a bore. One suspects that American scientists listened eagerly to his research pronouncements and at best feigned interest in his speeches on social reform. As a philanthropist, he was, after all, a leading patron of science in the new nation. Robert Owen shook the dust of New Harmony from his feet and left muttering about Maclure's educational plans as the arch saboteurs of Owen's hoped-for new social order on the banks of the Wabash. For Owen Senior, Maclure was insufferably contentious. For Robert Dale Owen, however, Maclure was accorded the esteem due to one who frees a son from intellectual dependence upon his father. To Joseph Neef he was a beloved patron; and to Thomas Say, the pioneer conchologist, Maclure was a Hebrew prophet. To all who knew him he was a man possessed by faith in education as the key to the Good Society.

JONATHAN BALDWIN TURNER:
PROPHETIC HERETIC IN HIGHER EDUCATION

The architects of grand designs are commonly less well remembered than are those who bring designs to fruition. The foreign policy statement framed largely by John Quincy Adams is remembered as James Monroe's Doctrine. The powerful influence once exerted upon the major political parties by such minor party forces as the Populists is easily forgotten. Seldom remembered are individuals like James G. Carter of Massachusetts who dropped into obscurity after working almost singlehandedly to create the office of secretary of the State Board of Education and to enlist public support for educational reform. Horace Mann, who so ably filled that office and used that support, alone won a place in history.

The Monroes, the major party chieftains, and the Manns stood, as Isaac Newton expressed his indebtedness, upon the shoulders of their own giants. In the history of American higher education Jonathan Baldwin Turner (1805-1899) was one of those obscure giants. David D. Henry, president of the University of Illinois, aptly noted in 1961 that Turner was a John the Baptist of the land grant college movement.[58] Justin Morrill, United States Senator from Vermont, earned deserved credit for sponsoring the successful land grant college bill that bore his name as the Morrill Land Grant Act of 1862. But Turner, a one-time professor of classics and *belles-lettres* in Illinois, along with such men as Henry Tappan of Michigan and Francis Wayland of Rhode Island, was also a prominent agitator for the reformation of higher education.

Turner's story might well have been told in connection with the earlier account of the Cooper, Lindsley, and Holley efforts to create archetypical state universities in antebellum America. In their battles to secularize and incorporate the newer sciences in higher education they could well have used such an ally as Turner. But Turner had far more Jacksonian exuberance than Jeffersonian restraint and his commitment to equal opportunities for all Americans far overshadowed his enthusiasm for scholarship per se, or, as Franklin expressed it, for "ornamental" studies.

In temperament and tenacity, moreover, if not in *weltanschauung*, Turner bore a most striking similarity to William Maclure. Geographically, little more than the Wabash River separated Turner from Maclure's New Harmony colleagues; and intellectually, Turner and Maclure drew similarly close battle-lines in their fights for educational reform. Both men saw society divided into two classes, although Turner's assessment of these classes was far more benign. Both men argued for a "modern" curriculum that would provide the larger class, the "producers" or, as Turner preferred, the "industrious" with "precisely the same principles of mental discipline and thorough scientific practical instruction, in all their pursuits and interests, which are now applied to the professional and military classes";[59] and they shared an impatience with those "consumers" or, again as Turner preferred, the "professionals" who denigrated all studies not clearly classical and mathematical. Each man preached a gospel of work that had the effect of supporting notions of man as *homo faber;* and both men were aghast to behold the rise of the corporation and its success in gaining legal definition as an individual. Democratic conceptions of equality guided both men.

Although Turner and Maclure were cast in a similar mold, important areas of disagreement stamped uniqueness upon each man. Maclure, like Horace Mann in this instance, held that the educational reformation should begin with the common school, whereas Turner consistently argued that "neither knowledge nor water will run up hill."[60] First he charged men to remold the higher institutions so that they might give a sense of direction to common schools, provide academically literate teachers, and through research, invention, and innovation promote human welfare and wisdom. And unlike Maclure, who devoted little attention to preparing teachers for the schools, and Mann, who preferred to promote normal schools as single-purpose institutions apart from the college and university, Turner argued prophetically for the university as a multipurpose institution which would also assume responsibility for teacher preparation. He combatted a persistent and dangerous naivete among American laymen about public education by arguing that "Money, however much or little, concentrated in logs, clapboards, and brick, inclosing a herd of listless, uneasy, and mischievous children, cannot make a common school." Seek first the qualified teacher! Let one's first financial commitment be made in recognition of the teacher as the keystone of sound education. "The living teacher must be there—living, not dead; for dead teachers only make dead scholars the more dead."[61] Let the reformed secular university guide and improve the development of the common schools; let it provide the schools with "competent and efficient teachers in the normal department of our industrial universities."[62] Ultimately, Turner stood with Maclure and Mann in his appreciation of the common school as "our great end, or last hope and final joy"; but he looked to a modern university, teaching applied sciences in all fields, as "the crowning glory of our common-school system."[63]

In pursuit of his objectives Turner's rebelliousness resembled Maclure's. Unlike Horace Mann, Maclure and Turner held little respect for the idea of conciliation. Confident of their rhetorical powers of persuasion, convinced that their causes were just, and themselves not tied to institutional procedures and restraints, Maclure and Turner consciously donned the gadfly's garb and paraded principle as conspicuously and precariously as a chip on the shoulder. Like Maclure, then, Turner was a rebel. His father Asa had served Daniel Shays in his famous rebellion and the son likewise supported the right as he saw it, regardless of the law. Whether the issue was education, sectarianism, slavery, or corporate abuses, Turner's argument remained essentially the same: "The first thing we need to do is to abate some of our stupid reverence for the law *as it is,* and begin really to inquire after the law as it *ought to be.*"[64] Turner's stubborn idealism emerged in his disdain for compromise and acquiescence and in his stiff-necked preference for head-on confrontations with opponents of Rightness; and it endeared him to many of his fellow Illinois frontiersmen. Here, they could be sure, was a college professor, and a Yale man at that, who knew how to combine eloquence with shirt-sleeves oratory and "common sense" in support of the common man and human progress.

Turner began his Illinois career quietly enough. In 1833 he reached Jacksonville and Illinois College, pledged to bring "religion and learning" to the American frontier. But the young professor did not long remain quiet. Over the next fourteen years as he preached, taught at the college, farmed, and recruited students he became a well-known and controversial partisan in burning issues, public and academic. In and beyond Illinois he argued for increased educational investments and opportunities for the "practical man." In and of itself this plea was merely nonsensical to many Illini but respectable among Turner's Congregational and Presbyterian colleagues. They supported denominational traditions that already had well-earned reputations as allies of education. But Turner coupled his advocacy of education in the new "sciences" to a disturbing departure from orthodoxy. His theological views and his tendency toward secularism became an embarrassment to Congregationalists and Presbyterians with whom he labored. He not only balked at predestination and the doctrine of election, he publicly hoped that human freedom would be accorded unlimited scope by "exterminating" notions of human depravity "from the face of the earth."[65] His relations with Illinois College became brittle, then broke irreparably over his attacks upon slavery and the Fugitive Slave Law. Discouraged and bedeviled, Turner resigned from Illinois College in 1847.

Thenceforth he was to embarrass no parent institution. In exchange for his position at the college the firebrand reformer gained the freedom he needed. He soon began to make his most telling indictments of sectarianism, slavery, and school inadequacies.

During the 1850's Turner led a concerted lobby effort to induce the Illinois legislature to establish an "Industrial University." His dream of educational reformation "from the top down" called for a national land grant act that would enable every state to provide "an APPROPRIATE LIBERAL EDUCATION" for its "INDUSTRIAL" class as well as for its "PROFESSIONAL" class.[66] While assessments of Turner's direct contributions to the Morrill Act must remain tentative and inconclusive, however laudatory, his impact upon the power structure of his own adopted state was of telling significance. As the leader of the Industrial League of Illinois he lectured, pamphleteered, formed political alliances, and corresponded persuasively with men of pivotal importance. Turner's success (and that of his associates) hinged heavily upon his ability to amplify the rustle of a minority movement until it seemed to become the roar of a popular upheaval in support of his proposed university. Few opportunities to reach the farmer and mechanic were missed; and every method of communication was employed exhaustively. (What more might a Maclure have accomplished had he understood the political nature of the American as clearly as did Mann and Turner?) Gradually Turner's plan won the hearty endorsement of the wealthy entrepreneurs, especially in Chicago, and some evidence of support from the working classes, so self-consciously suspicious of collegiate education, began to show itself as in the agricultural publications. By 1853, indeed, Turner found himself invited to ride the trains as the guest of the railroads wherever he went to promote his educational project. Only a few years earlier his views had cost him his professorship and his future seemed at best uncertain.

What was the substance of this university proposal that so aroused Illinois leadership? At Granville, Illinois, in 1851, Turner delivered an early outline of his plan for a state university that would serve primarily to systematize and teach the laboring classes "the true philosophy—the science and the art of their several pursuits (their life-business), and of efficiently applying existing knowledge thereto . . . , which the professional classes have long enjoyed in their pursuits."[67] Turner asserted that the millstone of tradition had too easily led men to equate higher education with little else but expertise in law, medicine, and theology, with studies that, in Turner's mid-nineteenth-century estimation, attracted roughly one per cent of the manpower of society. This one per cent of the population comprised the "professional classes." They were supposed to be the "laborious thinkers" and for them higher education seemed relevant. But where and how were "thinking laborers" to be prepared? The vast majority in society, the "industrial classes," seemed to be answering: "In the school of hard knocks." Recognizing only that colleges as they then functioned offered inadequate incentive to them, the laboring classes made the easy but tragically misguided leap to conclude that higher education per se was the bastion of esoteric irrelevance for the nation's workers. Turner suggested that the professional class itself had encouraged this fiction. Many of its members held that existing patterns of higher education afforded complete and unimpeachable exercises for mental discipline; and they concluded that since only a few students matriculated with success, therefore the mass of mankind might lack proper mental credentials for advanced studies. Traditionally trained educators "have ever deemed the liberal culture of the industrial classes an impossibility; for they have never tried nor even conceived of any other way of educating them except that by which they are rendered totally unfit for their several callings in after life."[68] And that was the point Turner pounced upon. A way did exist to make men fit for their several callings. A possible program of relevant advanced studies for the laboring classes needed only public support to become a reality. For the 99 per cent of society who comprised the "industrious" class Turner recommended a

> system of *liberal education* for their own class, and adapted to their own pursuits; to create for them an INDUSTRIAL LITERATURE, adapted to their professional wants, to raise up for them *teachers* and *lecturers,* for subordinate institutes, and to elevate them, their pursuits, and their posterity to that relative position in human society for which God designed them.[69]

His argument for a state university thus followed from at least four major premises and commitments. First, Turner declared that there existed ample raw material out of which to fashion formal studies for the working classes, studies that would stress the necessary interplay among abstract theory, controlled experimentation, and direct application. Studies covering "all possible knowledge and all modes and phases of science, abstract, mixed and practical" would be offered.[70] At present they were admittedly inchoate sciences. The paucity of rigorous scholarship and literature in these fields, however, could be overcome with high profit to society on university campuses dedicated to pursue knowledge in these fields. While the curriculum of the professionals' colleges had been studied "till trifles and fooleries have been magnified into matters of immense importance, and tornadoes of windy words and barrels of innocent ink [have been] shed over them in vain," the vast significance of principles underlying the mundane affairs of *homo faber* had only begun to dawn upon society.[71]

Turner here was turning his back squarely upon his alma mater. He argued in effect that the famous Yale Report of 1828 was an absurdity. In the face of challenging changes in the curricula and prescribed studies at Harvard and some of the new colleges the Yale faculty had in that year issued a ringing defense of a traditional pattern of higher learning, a pattern Turner himself had followed as a student. True, the program of studies at Yale did not directly prepare one for most of the careers open to him, but by design, not as an oversight. The proper function of collegiate education in the judgment of the Yale faculty was to provide the student with a necessary introduction to the enduring problems created out of man's need to understand the human predicament. More important, perhaps, the classical curriculum alone afforded the mental discipline prerequisite to subsequent specialization in any field of human enterprise. Without naming his own school, Turner rapped the Yale Report assertions with unrestrained delight. If the classical curriculum "produces infallible practical reasoners," he pondered, "we have a great many thousand infallible antagonistic truths, and ten thousand conflicting paths of right, interest, duty and salvation."[72] He then countered with an assertion of his own: "The most natural and effectual mental discipline possible for any man, arises from setting him to earnest and constant thought about things he daily does, sees, and handles, and all their connected relations and interests."[73] The new university would teach useful studies and thereby provide the means for a superior discipline of the reasoning powers of man.

Second, Turner argued that the proposed university would put an end to the endemic "common sense" and rule-of-thumb approaches to richly complex arenas of human endeavor. Sadly, society had not yet fully realized that its workers needed advanced and specialized education. Turner charged:

> As things now are our best farmers and mechanics, by their own native force of mind, by the slow process of individual experience, come to know, at forty, what they might have been taught in six months at twenty; while a still greater number of the less fortunate or less gifted, stumble on through life, almost as ignorant of every true principle of their art as when they begun [*sic*]. A man of real skill is amazed at the slovenly ignorance and waste he everywhere discovers, . . . and still more to hear . . . [workers] boast of their ignorance of all "bookfarming". . . .

In anticipation of those who would reply that "their children can do as well as . . . [their parents] have done," Turner exclaimed that "it certainly would be a great pity if they could not."[74] Turner's proposed university would attract only the intelligent worker able to see the necessity of uniting theory and practice. Those too ignorant to see the superiority of systematic study of human endeavors to the waste and squalor bred out of a union of bare intuition and rules-of-thumb would not be found among the university's students or patrons. But they would be soon sent scurrying by their university-trained competitors.

Third, Turner pictured his proposed university as a political balance wheel stabilizing and perpetuating democratic life in the nation. Here he echoed Bacon—and Maclure. Knowledge is power. An imbalance in the dissemination of knowledge produces like imbalance in the body politic. Turner believed that higher education only for lawyers, doctors, and clergymen would produce a powerful threat to the legitimate interests of *"all men of all classes."*

> If any one class provide for their own liberal education in the state, *as they should do,* while another class neglect this, it is as inevitable as the law of gravitation, that they should form a ruling caste or class by themselves, and wield their power more or less for their own exclusive interests and the interests of their friends.[75]

Thus "liberal education," as broadly redefined, would serve a threefold purpose: It would humanize the thought and labor of the industrial class; it would thereby enable that 99 per cent of society to make more worthy contributions to national progress; and liberal education for all would serve the long-range goal of forestalling the danger, whether the creature of design or default, of an educated elite in the land.

Turner's fourth premise for the new university was that academic leadership should come from within the industrial class itself. He had already laid to rest the plea of the Yale Report for general education based on a traditional curriculum. From there Turner moved to the obvious conclusion that spokesmen for the professional class should neither guide the destiny of the new university nor be permitted to force upon students the whimsical speculations of politics and religion. Here he echoed Maclure. In the interests of greater democracy and in keeping with constitutional restraints against church-state union, Turner viewed the state university as a secular and nonpartisan public institution. Here again he agreed with Maclure rather than with Mann.

> No species of knowledge should be excluded [from the pro-
> posed university], practical or theoretical; unless, indeed,
> those specimens of "organized ignorance" found in the
> creeds of party politicians, and sectarian ecclesiastics should
> be mistaken by some for a species of knowledge.[76]

He acknowledged that some persons

> may feel a little alarm, when, for the first time in the history
> of the world, they see the millions throwing themselves aloof
> from all political and ecclesiastical control, and attempting
> to devise a system of liberal education for themselves: but
> on mature reflection we trust they will approve the plan; or
> if they are too old to change, their children will.[77]

II

Mann, Maclure, and Turner attempted to fashion models of
the common school ideal at a time when no one clearly foresaw
the implications of a single ladder of public education extending
from earliest formal training to higher education. None of these
three men, for example, saw the singular significance of the public
high school. By 1860 it was still but a small threat to the private
academies that then provided the most substantial link between the
common school and the college. The rise of the public university
after the Civil War contributed in no small measure to the efforts
to pry open the public purse in the interests of free secondary
education for American youth.

While the aim and organization of the public high school became a central pedagogical issue after 1890, descriptions of the
purposes of common school education had found widespread acceptance before the Civil War. The school was responsible for basic
literacy and arithmetical calculation; it was to combine lessons in
morality with learning as a character-building institution; and it
would induce patriotism through studies designed to promote
civic competence. Widespread agreement about the school's areas
of responsibility, however, signaled only that the idea of the common school had been translated into reality. Controversy thenceforth centered primarily upon the procedural steps to be taken by
the school in fulfilling its responsibilities. The methods by which
patriotism and morality, especially, should be transmitted to youth
have become major targets of criticism.

Horace Mann's attempt to forestall this criticism through the
"common elements" as presented by teachers blessed with fine
impartiality has never won steady support from the American tax-
payers, but the general impact of his educational ideals has made

him a major prophet of the course of the common schools. William Maclure, who fought indoctrination, formalism, and day schools, was to become at best a minor prophet. Views similar to his perhaps survive in certain private boarding schools of the twentieth century, but rather by accident than by conscious appropriation of his ideas. His struggles against nationalism in education and for acceptance of the idea of the school as reform-bent critic of society ring, even to the most receptive ears, as anachronisms.

Although Jonathan Baldwin Turner also actively campaigned to strengthen common school education in Illinois, his place in history rests with his agitation in behalf of the land grant college idea. He was anticipated and joined by several reformers. Certainly Thomas Jefferson, Thomas Cooper, Philip Lindsley, and Horace Holley gave lasting momentum to this early impulse. At first too unsteady and uncertain in its direction to be a movement, battles to establish universities that would be responsive to public interests gradually gave rise to certain trends in the development of state universities. Private and quasi-public universities have also often followed similar lines of development, but in public mind the state university and the following trends have become most consciously linked.

Among the most far-reaching of these trends has been that toward a secular attitude concerning, first, knowledge in general and, ultimately, morality as well. A greater emphasis on secular knowledge has marked the activities of all kinds of institutions, although religiously oriented colleges have tended to resist secular standards of morality.[78] The machinery of public control established for some of the early state universities led, for brief periods, to a kind of balance of powers among ideological groups. Those who with Turner, Cooper, Lindsley, and Holley took advantage of these brief periods to assert the superiority of secular canons were subject to incessant charges of "godlessness," and though often defeated in the end, they were, in a sense, the pioneers of secularism.

A second major trend has emphasized the service function of higher education. To use a mid-twentieth-century term coined, it is thought, by President Pusey of the non-state university at Cambridge, higher education has tried to render "service without servility." Speaking of this function with respect to the development of the state universities after the Civil War, James Bryce saw them as "the mind of the State, or at least the organ which the State may employ to examine and think out the problems which the State has to deal with."[79] The service function, Bryce noted,

> has the merit of associating all the citizens in a direct and personal way with the university, making them feel it to be

their creation, arousing the liberality of the legislature to it, and giving the whole State an interest in its prosperity and efficiency.[80]

This very closeness to the citizenry gave the university, in the opinion of the historian Frederick Jackson Turner,

> a peculiar power in the direct influence upon the whole people and a peculiar limitation in its dependence upon the people. The ideals of the people constitute the atmosphere in which it moves, though it can itself affect this atmosphere. Herein is the source of its strength and the direction of its weakness. Nothing in our educational history [Turner maintained] is more striking than the steady pressure of democracy upon its universities to adapt them to the requirements of all the people.[81]

That the service function had led to servility in the state universities was argued most bluntly in the twentieth century by Norman Foerster, the noted Neo-Humanist:

> The American state university has progressively tended to subvert the higher interests of American democracy. It has devoted itself to ends that are not ends, to truths that are only half-truths, to services that have turned out to be disservices, to practicalities that have become impracticalities and absurdities.[82]

But whether the danger of servility to false ends be seen through the eyes of Jonathan Baldwin Turner, Cooper, Lindsley, Holley, Frederick Jackson Turner, or Norman Foerster, the state universities have developed a structure distinctively geared to service, and have led the trend in this direction. It is well to ask if those communities which early used the machinery of a state university exercised the kind of restraint needed if universities are to retain sufficient autonomy.

A third trend, the extension of educational opportunity to an ever-widening portion of the populace, was both cause and effect of the service emphasis. The belief that education, if not a universal panacea, was at least a cure for social class immobility found expression in all American educational institutions as the nineteenth century progressed. As the capstone of the public school system the state university provided, it was argued, the critical test of commitment to equality of opportunity. According to Frederick Jackson Turner, the public school system, and particularly the state university, fosters

> that due degree of individualism which is implied in the
> right of every human being to have opportunity to rise in
> whatever directions his peculiar abilities entitle him to go,
> subordinate to the welfare of the state. It keeps the avenues
> of promotion to the highest offices, the highest honors, open
> to the humblest and most obscure lad who has the natural
> gifts, at the same time that it aids in the improvement of
> the masses.[83]

The new frontiers whose unlimited resources were to provide the
all-important opportunities for social and economic mobility were
to be opened by the universities. In Turner's words, "The test tube
and the microscope are needed rather than ax and rifle in this new
ideal of conquest."[84]

A fourth trend in which the state universities participated, an
extension of research and instruction into a wider field of inquiry,
was also partly rooted in the desire for service and opportunity;
but not only here. The memory of the great professional schools of
the medieval universities, and the Baconian assumption that knowledge is power and is capable of continuous advancement, were
much in the minds of Enlightenment thinkers. Such ideas led them
to talk grandly of great national universities and academies in
which mature and highly skilled scholars would assault the fortress
of the unknown. At the very moment of disillusionment with the
French *philosophes*, Americans discovered the new German universities which re-enforced the ideal of catholicity of instruction
and research. As will be seen in the following chapter the German
university ideal and drive for *kulture* also revived academic notions
of a Good Society based upon education. At any event, the new
studies demanded by American life augmented those suggested by
European experience.

These four trends made a fifth inevitable. Secular knowledge
in the areas where its extension was demanded is expensive. Experimental facilities, farms, hospitals, laboratory schools, and shops
were vastly more costly than the limited classical libraries formerly
required. The increased length of formal schooling, and the expanding population demanding this schooling, compounded the
problem of support—never an easy one to solve. The state university expected an increasing portion of the community to help
in paying the pipers; naturally more tunes were called for. An in-
flationary cycle in educational costs was under way.

Much of the story of American higher education can be told
in terms of these five trends. The history of the state universities
is the record of their peculiar set of responses. By the end of the
nineteenth century a reasonably stable structure had evolved. By

the 1960's, however, one could find in such phenomena as the community college, the University of the State of New York, and the state college and university system of California, evidence that the structure was again rapidly changing. The stories of Turner, Cooper, Lindsley, and Holley unfolded in a time when a few men, in a few communities, were locked in struggles that shaped the responses that came to characterize the later state universities.

In like manner, much of the story of American elementary and secondary education can be told in terms of unsteady consensus about the meaning of "common elements" of learning for all American youth. Almost unanimously embraced and defended, the American common school has at the same time ever been entangled in debates about the nature and suitable procedures for teaching "common elements."

The debates have been particularly vigorous with respect to efforts to find literature appropriate to inculcate moral values. From Horace Mann to Dwight D. Eisenhower large numbers of Americans have believed that morality rests ultimately on a deep religious faith. Yet literature adequate to express, and methods adequate to inculcate, the faith of one group have proved anathema to others. Thus Horace Mann believed that the "common elements of Christianity" could be taught by ritually reading from the King James Bible without comment. Roman Catholic leaders agitated for a half-century before some state courts ruled that such use of the Bible constituted a sectarian and therefore uncommon bias, a bias destructive of the religious liberty guaranteed all Americans under the Constitution. Not until 1963 did the United States Supreme Court arrive at the same conclusion. When it so ruled in the cases of Abington *v.* Schempp and Murray *v.* Curlett, cries of distress were heard throughout the land.

As public schoolmen sought a formulation acceptable to all groups, the common elements of Protestant Christianity became the common elements of Christianity, then the Judeo-Christian ethic, and finally the traditions of Western Civilization. As part of that tradition it was still possible, according to the 1963 decision, to study the Bible and religion so long as they were " . . . presented objectively as part of a secular program of education. . . . " Such a study reflects, however, much more the idea of William Maclure who believed the school should present only facts than that of Horace Mann who considered the Bible the source of ultimate Truth. Two other controversies challenge the concepts of integration and segregation of students in quest of "common elements." One, supported by enlightened sentiment and the historic (and unanimous) United States Supreme Court decision of 1954, struck down statutory support for the practice of segregating school children on the basis of their race. The other controversy arose over proposals that intellectually gifted students be segregated in special sessions rather than remain in classes that represent a broader sampling of average American youth. "Once again," as Lawrence Cremin reminds us, "the issue becomes one inherently connected with the historic effort to maintain a school common to all the children of all the people."[85] And once again, the issue becomes one inseparable from arguments about the concept of community.

•

CHAPTER THREE

Pangloss and the Primitive

•

Sometimes I think they'se poison in th' life iv a big city. Th' flowers won't grow here no more thin they wud in a tannery, an' th' bur-rds have no song; an' th' childher iv dacint men an' women come up hard in th' mouth an' with their hands raised again their kind.

FINLEY PETER DUNNE

The child should learn the adjustment of himself to the world that already exists. . . . He shall learn institutions and reconcile himself to them. . . . He must learn to see their rationality.

WILLIAM T. HARRIS

For most of us, the best education is that which makes us the best and most obedient servants.

G. STANLEY HALL

"Solomon says,—explicitly and without qualification,—'Train up a child in the way he should go, and when he is old, HE WILL NOT DEPART FROM IT.'"[1] Horace Mann had enthusiastically endorsed Solomon's instructions. This straightforward scriptural order helped Mann drive home an impression of education as profoundly important—and reasonably uncomplicated.

If the community possessed the will to establish and sustain schools it could unlock the moral power of learning. The schools would prove to be the test of the community, of its willingness to invest in virtue, intelligence, and in the prospects of a more humane posterity. If a wise parent could listen profitably to Solomon, so too could the wise community carefully and systematically straighten twigs to make their trees stand more nobly. In Mann's era, when free and universal day school education was still largely a vision, it seemed axiomatic that education was a weapon upon which only the forces of Good would dare rely. It hardly occurred to many of his contemporaries that schools might simply perpetuate regnant inequity, petty meanness, and hypocrisy. To warn that education could ably serve any and all ideological ends was to hazard the brand of an enemy of the common schools.

By the end of the nineteenth century the vision of common schools across the land had become all but settled fact. But many signs unhappily suggested that either Americans had placed excessive hopes in the meliorative powers of education or they had too widely subverted and scarcely tapped that power. In such an ambivalent mood the scholar Henry Seidel Canby ruefully recalled his own village childhood in the 1890's. His home town, and through it his home-town school, had been dominated (if not domineered) by a commercially sound religious ethic and had sung the praises of "hard work" and "success." The community-school coalition had made Canby and his classmates "in its own likeness and we were exactly fitted to its narrow philistinism." The school had trained up the child, to be sure, as Solomon had advised, but with a blunted sense of the way in which he should go. The school, like the town, was "blind and dumb esthetically and rather proud of it."[2] To observers sensitive as Canby it seemed to mirror all too faithfully the complacent myopia of late nineteenth-century small towns before the spectacle of portentous transformations in the conditions of American life. Had Canby never left home his assessment might have been far more laudatory. It would certainly have been less perceptive. In all likelihood, indeed, it would not have been set forth as a formal essay. But Canby did leave home. The city beckoned him as it began to beckon other Canbys of his day. Increasing numbers of ambitious and talented youth sought their futures in the metropolitan meccas. They represented one of many signs that the small towns were no longer to set the patterns of American life.

In the cities, the great new centers of commerce, industry, and struggling culture, Solomon's saying collided with even more profoundly disturbing social facts. Where were the family, church, school, and business patterns so clearly visible and consciously perpetuated in the small town? Who now trained up the child, and for what purpose? If the city was a place of greater promise, it was also a place of greater peril for education. Commerce, not learning, had accounted most heavily for the amazing growth of cities following the Civil War. The rise of the cities and the rise of American industrial might are therefore two closely related stories. Each giant stride taken by American industry after 1865 left new mills and enlarged cities, coal pits and more cities, factories and mushrooming cities again. New conditions of employment, new forms of family and neighborhood life, appeared to vex man in pursuit of a Good Society.

Immigration accounted for much of the urban trend and crucial demographic changes. A hint of the impact of immigration appeared when approximately two-and-one-half million newcomers arrived during each of the decades of the 1850's, 1860's, and 1870's. The figure for the 1880's, suddenly and prophetically, rose into a human floodtide of more than five million. Once it had been the lure of a common man's utopia, based on images of a land of physical and spiritual freedom, that brought foreigners mainly from Northern and Western Europe. Now, more so than in earlier decades, many foreigners came in response to outside pressures; and American industrialists launched labor recruiting campaigns abroad. Vastly increased numbers of the more lingually, socially, and politically handicapped members of Eastern and Southern European and Asian communities came to America.

Many of these fresh sources of manpower for American technological might streamed into the cities. Ignorant of English and representative government, destitute, huddled in ghettoes, stacked in tenements, unorganized and eager to work for a pittance, they became the natural enemy of an indigenous American labor force and an overwhelming consternation to humanitarians, patriotic and charitable organizations, clergymen, and educators. Americans thanked France for her gift of the Statue of Liberty and hastened off to urge already anxious legislators to apply curbs and quotas upon immigrants. One interest group after another decried the new waves of foreigners as carriers of anarchism, socialism, filth, polygamy, prostitution, and a host of similar and sometimes surprising evils. But the foreigners were here and continued to come. The city became an arena for demographic dilemmas and for the sometimes brutal battles of "assimilation" and "Americanization."

Thus for a host of reasons, life in the city came to be seen as distinct, especially in a qualitative sense, from earlier American social experience. The noted Chicago editor and humorist Finley Peter Dunne let "Mr. Dooley" speak for many: "Sometimes I think they'se poison in th' life iv a big city. Th' flowers won't grow here no more thin they wud in a tannery, an' th' bur-rds have no song; an' th' childher iv dacint men an' women come up hard in th'

mouth an' with their hands raised again their kind."[3] Sprawling
to accommodate more commerce, industry, and widening streams
of newcomers, American and foreign, the great new cities thus provided a disturbing informal education of their own. Many youngsters, struck full by the perils of squalor and pleasures of wealth,
learned that one must run or be trampled. The child's world of
stones, steel, and smoke furnished the lessons he received from
"Nature." This new world was the natural habitat of those who
received the most lavish rewards and the most severe punishments
meted out by the "bitch goddess, Success."

There was misery to match the majesty of a great nation coming of age. If we have dilated upon the former, it is because its
depth and dimension, to a marked degree, set the tone and ground
rules of the educational debates of the early twentieth century.
What could men hope to do about the fact of human misery?
Surely this too would pass away, heal over, with time. That all
societies changed, no informed person could doubt. In this sense,
at least, Darwinian principles of evolution seemed to support older
popular Enlightenment postulates. Some national leaders hotly
disputed the wisdom of conscious attempts, in the spirit of Enlightenment optimism, to control or force change. William Graham
Sumner enjoyed influential support for his contention that men
should not meddle with the human predicament. In the eighteenth century Alexander Pope had argued, "WHATEVER IS, IS
RIGHT." Sumner argued, in effect, that whatever is, is. He attempted
to move the discussion above the question of right and wrong to
stress the futility of reform. "The great stream of time and earthly
things will sweep on just the same in spite of us," he concluded.
"It is only in imagination that we stand by and look at and criticize
it and plan to change it. Everyone of us is . . . in the stream and is
swept along with it."[4]

William James also doubted that reform would produce social
perfection and agreed tacitly with Sumner that life was a prolonged
confrontation with uncertainties. But he was temperamentally
unsuited to accept Sumner's deterministic fatalism. He could not
tolerate the notion "that our hopes and desires are misfits in the
scheme of things."[5] James steadfastly insisted "That the course of
destiny may be altered by individuals no wise evolutionist ought to
doubt."[6] Man could in fact create a better state; he could live the
life of meliorism *if* "a *divided* universe be a conception possible for
his intellect to rest in, and at the same time he have the vigor of will
to look the universal death in the face, without blinking. . . ."[7]
An ideal state of sorts, one with "vice there, and virtue holding her
by the throat," stood for James within the realm of human possibility.[8]

How then and to what extent should the school be expected to participate in the attempt to throttle vice and liberate creative intelligence? What was the relationship of rational thought to genetic impulse in determining human behavior? To what sort of community life ought man aspire, and what was the function of the schools with respect to community life? These and other questions were loudly debated in educational circles, particularly at the meetings of the National Educational Association, then in its golden age so far as the participation of distinguished college and public school educators was concerned. For two decades such men as Charles Eliot of Harvard, Nicholas Murray Butler of Columbia, William T. Harris, first as St. Louis' school superintendent and later as U. S. Commissioner of Education, and G. Stanley Hall, professor of psychology at Johns Hopkins and later President of Clark University tried to chart the course of American education for the coming twentieth century.

Among the sharpest differences were those between Harris and Hall: the former an apologist for laissez faire and an exponent of the development of intellectual powers as the fundamental purpose of the school; the latter a utopian social thinker and exponent of the life of instinct and passion. Harris' view of the proper social order as well as his view of human nature was early and fully set forth; Hall argued about human nature, curriculum, and pedagogy, but for years camouflaged his views of the good society.

I

THE LAISSEZ-FAIRE STATE AND EDUCATION

Between 1889 and 1906 William Torrey Harris held a position of high political visibility in American education. As the United States Commissioner of Education during that period, Harris moved from the realm of regional importance to the arena of national prominence. He had gained recognition as the nation's foremost authority on Hegel; and as Commissioner of Education he worked to strengthen his grasp on this field. As founder and editor of the pioneering *Journal of Speculative Philosophy* (1867) he had afforded an impressive circle of dilettantes and academicians with an important outlet for their creative endeavor. He had worked his way steadily through the ranks of the educational pyramid in St. Louis, Missouri, between 1857-1867. After having served as a teacher, principal, and assistant superintendent, Harris, in that latter year and until 1880, held the office of superintendent of the St. Louis schools. Here under his auspices emerged what is presumed to be the first public kindergarten in the United States.

From the cosmic heights of speculative philosophy to the laying of plans for the pre-school child, Harris seemed a most appropriately endowed man for the clearing-house job of Commissioner.

In a formal sense the office in Washington, D. C., served the American schools in a delicately indirect and limited capacity, one primarily of analysis, statistical service, and monographic inquiry into educational processes. Informally, however, the office provided an important halo effect which, then as now, meant more impressive speaking engagements, more eager publishers, and related opportunities to influence educational policies. From this position his educational views attracted wide attention. Harris worked, for example, to stem the rising interest in the sciences. The place of science in public education was, he reasoned, subordinate to the social sciences and humanities. His voice thus rose in opposition to American disciples of Herbert Spencer who, in response to his own question "What Knowledge is of Most Worth?" had answered: "Science." To those who drew inspiration from the idea that the school should be a microcosmic community Harris inveighed against any attempt by schoolmen to assume responsibilities that belonged to the family, state, church, and business. He denounced the notion that teachers should expect favors in the form of exemption from the rules of business enterprise. Teachers were to be paid according to the laws of supply and demand, with wage determination to be in part based upon the assumptions that (1) male teachers merit more than females and (2) effective teaching at the higher grades is more difficult than at the lower grades. And it also followed that (3) administrators were worth more than teachers—of either sex.

Far beyond the mysterious intricacies of educational processes and administration Harris spoke as "a champion of industrial capitalism and the virtues that it prized."[9] In support of "rugged individualism" he made tireless replies to critics of capitalism from left and right. He pleaded cogently against the views of socialists, isolationists, against Henry George and Karl Marx. The American State, the best yet to write its story in the book of institutional evolution, was fundamentally sound. Its major institutions, identified as government, family, church, business, and education, were by impressive degrees gradually transforming national society into more ethically and spiritually pure form. Harris's Hegelian frame of reference regularly guided his carefully phrased defenses of the world-as-it-is. He did not deny that serious problems faced the nation. Immigrants, agrarian problems, slums, labor strife, and urban and industrial dislocations admittedly posed problems; but Harris had long since firmly concluded that social criticism was neither philosophically proper nor socially responsible.

His favorite novel, one that he argued would be most profitably read by American youth, was Goethe's *Wilhelm Meister*. All youth should learn the lesson of *Meister*, that the individual's sense of estrangement from society simply betrayed his own inadequacies. One's struggle for freedom could be successful only when the State was recognized as the supreme agent of human freedom. In Harris's estimation, Goethe taught youth to begin "at the bottom of the ladder" and climb into an awareness and acceptance of the State as his rightful spiritual parent. The individual thereby learned "the adjustment of himself to the world that already exists. . . . He shall learn institutions and reconcile himself to them . . . he must learn to see their rationality . . . ."[10] With Hegel's sanguine teleology supporting his systematic defenses of the status quo, Harris served as the Dr. Pangloss of the pedagogical world.

Without the State humanity was an impossibility; the child apart from State could become only a barbarian. His puerile interests, unless forged into alignment with State-provided motive force of Will, would make him a psychic slave. Estranged from society and alienated ultimately even from himself, man gropes in vain for freedom. In the States resides the wisdom of accumulated human experience. Freedom comes by hearing, and hearing by the laws of the State. Is creativity not built upon standards and rules? Is not true individuality built upon a realization of the wisdom of social conformity in matters of common interest? Is not the State man's best hope for union with the Universal Consciousness? Harris affirmed each question. The critical pedagogical maxim thus became clear: Man gained ultimate freedom in the State only by relinquishing all claim to it as a child. Rousseau, in one mood, had argued that the truly free man, the possessor of *amour de soi*, would have experienced a childhood carefully protected from the rational pursuits of the adult world. But Rousseau's argument had followed from the notion that "God makes all things good; man meddles with them and they become evil."[11] Harris turned Rousseau on his head by declaring, in effect, that the child's education must involve a conscious and expressly rational process of "self-estrangement" from his animal nature. Divine Will (as revealed in the institutions of the State) must set his tasks and be his master. His own interests were to be neither trusted nor guided. Man is not born good as Rousseau had maintained. Nor is he born free. He is born, Harris preferred to believe, in chains; but through allegiance to the institutions of his society he gains freedom. Thus is the child spared from becoming a "monster."[12]

The school was to develop that sense of allegiance. It was the agency depended upon by the State to alienate the child from the monster in his nature, develop the youngster's higher and spiritual nature, and teach him the high virtue of social harmony. To these ends his emotional nature, his "desires and affections," had to be controlled and diverted to the Good; through the inculcation of proper habits his will power required much development. Believing that the child possessed the ability to reason, Harris concluded that the tasks of the school could best be done by teachers who respect the child as a creature possessing vastly greater intellectual abilities than Rousseau and his beneficiaries believed. Upon leaving school the child should be able and eager to contribute to the mission of the State. His will and intellect should be at that juncture highly and equally developed. Harris insisted upon this balance. Man driven by will sans intellect amounted to a "mere machine"; and intellect without will reduced him to a "cipher."[13]

Harris's ideal curriculum carried a peculiarly modern ring. He sternly disagreed with his contemporaries who followed Francis W. Parker's romantic wing of educational reform, believing that the school should become "a model home, a complete community, and an embryonic democracy."[14] Such ideas, it seemed to Harris, tended to turn educators away from their special rationalistic tasks. Peripheral social factors thereby became central educational considerations. Concern for the "whole child" increased, while notions of the child as a reasoning creature became increasingly suspect. The "whole child" thus came surprisingly close to meaning a pedagogical interest in all the child's abilities and relationships with the exception of his intellectual attainment. Harris's curricular suggestions, linked to a faculty psychology even then sorely threatened by empirical data, aimed at correcting such alleged imbalances of the "new education" at the end of the nineteenth century.

Five study areas opened the "five windows of the soul" for the student. His studies of nature, inorganic and organic, would provide appreciation of the laws controlling the infrahuman world. The physical sciences, carried largely by arithmetic and mathematics, would be firmly placed in the school. Because they provided no great revelation of divinely inspired human purposes, however, they were subordinate to the life sciences which did reveal important clues to divine nature. These first two study areas suffered the severe limitation of being unable to address themselves to the great questions of human values. The last three windows of the soul, however—grammar, literature, and history—admitted the light of truth about the ethical and moral dimensions of existence. Especially in his support of grammar, Harris's adherence to faculty psychology became clear. Modern and classical language studies, he insisted, offered excellent disciplinary opportunities for the mind. They introduced the child to the structure of reason itself and cultivated those habits of mind necessarily possessed by philosophers. Literature (and art), then, contributed the most stirring and sound expressions of great human thought and sentiment; and thereby afforded exemplary human attempts to explain and transmit human values. Finally, history, and in that context the relevant cultural contributions of the emergent social sciences, would chronicle man's slow, but progressively successful, attempts to create the crowning embodiment of Universal Consciousness, the State. If one scissored away the rather tortuous teleology and mystifying metaphysical premise from which Harris began, one could hardly distinguish his prospectus for educational excellence from those preferred in the mid-1960's by critics of the fads and frills of American schools.

Harris's program provided a fascinating union of the spiritual and the mundane. If mathematics disciplined minds, it also readied the student for commerce by teaching him "the practical side of exchange." Geography developed understandings of the parent planet; and it also informed one of the status of international trade. With due attention to the ethical distinctions between good and evil, "Education must make the pupil capable of deciding on the *usefulness* of an object, by reference to its effect on his permanent vocation."[15] "Culture Study," grammar and literature, meanwhile, served as the primary vehicle for turning the child toward an appreciation of his own "ideal essence."[16] History, then, provided the clinching arguments for individual (and largely economic) initiative. Through history the child learned to admire and emulate the contributions of the "great men" whose lives stood as testaments to the wisdom of individualism; and, particularly through extended studies of the constitutional state, the child learned that the State is sacrosanct. Driven by will, determined to succeed as an individual in the world-as-it-is, uncritically loyal to the Laissez-Faire State as the true source of human freedom, the pupil gained the strength to "withstand wild schemes of agitation that attack radically all the institutions of civilization."[17] In a positive sense education was for Harris the agency that taught the child due respect for individualism as it prospered under the aegis of the remaining four institutions of the Laissez-Faire State: the family, government, church, and private enterprise. The school goaded him to excel according to extant rules. The "greatest glory of an educational system" was its ability to make the rising generation eager to embark upon State-protected competitions. In a comfortably economic mood, Harris rhetorically asked an audience of New Haven educators in 1882, "What place is there in our system for a drone who is utterly devoid of aspiration?"[18]

In his own way, Harris was no less an educational democrat than William Maclure or Jonathan Baldwin Turner. With them he assumed that proper nurture and education would abundantly justify faith in individual dignity and common schools. Where gross human inequities appeared, however, Maclure and Turner would point accusatively at institutional shortcomings. Harris at such moments invariably defended the institution. His sometimes murky and often bewildering Hegelian explications and the surprising ease with which he drifted back and forth between the *is-* and the *ought-*realms, affirmed anew that this was the best of all possible worlds. If the major premises seemed dim and distant the conclusion was etched with confident clarity. With typical piquancy William James confided that Harris "is to me simply preposterous, albeit a holy man." "He revolves like a squirrel in a cage in one circle of ideas; all openings presently lead into that circle, and then the monotonous whirring begins."[19]

Be that as it may, Harris was widely appreciated for his ability to give a most soothing and scholarly verbal massage to anxious Americans who had the greatest stakes in those institutions. If his vagueness annoyed or awed some, his earnest eloquence stood unmistakably recognized by many. His mission, after all, was taken to be inspirational and heuristic. Details he left to lesser minds. And he considered Maclure to be representative of those pedagogues who plodded between the blinders of technique and aimless detail. Looking back upon Maclure's New Harmony contributions, Harris concluded that Maclure

> laid so much stress on the mechanical features of education that he in a great measure neutralized the effect of the school on the characters of his pupils, for he more or less turned off the minds of his pupils from those studies which give original initiative, and turned them in the direction of matters of skill and routine practise.[20]

Maclure's response might well have been more pungent. But would the argument have been relevant? For all their differences both men still sustained the belief that all normal members of the human family shared the ability to reason. By the late nineteenth century, however, an impressive minority of influential Americans seemed to have found evidence that undercut not only faith in human reason but democracy itself, whether socialistic as Maclure wanted it or laissez faire as praised by Harris.

II

EVOLUTION AND THE UNCONSCIOUS

In the decades following the Civil War, the would-be architect of "scientific" education could well have abandoned belief in the primacy of reason. By 1900 he might have believed that questions raised by Darwinian theories of evolution and the "discovery" of the unconscious mind could not be answered from the fund of human knowledge drawn upon by Helvetius, the Owens, and Maclure. If "natural selection" and "survival of the fittest" were natural, ongoing evolutionary processes, then were not the inherited characteristics of the ever-evolving organism more important than its environment for this process? If the organism possessed a high order of vitality and power of adaptation would it not be more likely to overcome unfavorable factors in the environment? If it possessed more strength and cunning than its natural enemies would it not survive? Could not the history of genus *Homo* and the emergence of species *sapiens* be understood more clearly in this light?

Furthermore, did not evolutionary biological ideas encourage, even demand, greater emphasis on appetite, organic tendencies, and will as necessary foundations for reason? And were not they capable of generating life *without* reason? The "discovery" of unconscious factors in human conduct, which had become a popular conversation topic in many fashionable circles as early as 1870, seemed to affirm this suspicion.[21] Did man really reason, or did he just think that he reasoned? Did he act according to conscious and rational judgment, or did his senses play vicious tricks upon his ego while pulleys driven by the engines of his unconscious controlled his behavior? If adult behavior could be opened to such a question, what could be said for the behavior of children! Did youth reason at all? Or were they, like primitive man, probably incapable of reasoning and driven only by emotion and will? If the ability to reason was but a recent phenomenon in human evolution, was it not likely that many adults in contemporary society had not arrived at that exalted stage?

The social philosopher who could have converted each of these questions into a law or a working hypothesis would have felt the ideas of Mann, Maclure, and even Harris grating against his sensibilities. If the social philosopher had been Granville Stanley Hall (1844-1924), the first President of Clark University, he would have sought out a different set of intellectual forebears to draw upon in designing an appropriate educational program.

Hall looked for encouragement to Plato, who had been showered with abuse by so many nineteenth-century social reformers. He preferred the arguments of Rousseau to such materialistic and nakedly rational words as Maclure and Turner uttered, and preferred Pestalozzi's romantic picture of the village of Bonnal to the community of New Harmony. Because Hall placed will above reason in current human affairs he listened to Schopenhauer more carefully than to Jefferson or Paine. Because unconscionable pleas for equality and vicious in-fighting for dollar prizes highlighted human behavior for Hall during the late nineteenth century, he became convinced that most men were not yet reasoning creatures. He turned to theories of human evolution and joined Nietzsche's vigilant watch for a coming race of supermen to preserve his own faith in tomorrow.

A STRANGER IN ACADEME?

Granville Stanley Hall, an amazingly productive scholar in the fields of education and psychology, was the first man in the United States to receive the degree of doctor of philosophy in psychology, and he went on to become the inspiration of the phenomenal child-study movement. As the first president of Clark University he worked to outstrip Johns Hopkins in importing the Germanic model for university education. He organized the American Psychological Association and established and edited numerous scholarly journals. His list of professional publications included fourteen books and contained more than four hundred titles.[22]

In his last years, Hall had no time for modest protestations about his accomplishments:

> In the views I have attained of man, his place in nature, his origin and destiny, I believe I have become a riper product of the present stage of civilization than most of my contemporaries, have outgrown more superstitions, attained clearer insights, and have a deeper sense of peace with myself. I love but perhaps still more pity mankind, groping and stumbling, often slipping backward along the upward Path, which I believe I see just as clearly as Jesus or Buddha did. . . .[23]

To some of his professional colleagues, however, it remained debatable whether Hall was inspired or misguided. One colleague, S. C. Fisher, saw Hall in unscientific pursuit of some great idea. Hall was compared to a man who "sees whatever thought it is that possesses him pervading and explaining the universe; he becomes almost a prophet, a mystic, an arriver at ultimate reality. So far-reaching in its possible effects upon human happiness and self-knowledge does the idea—self-stripped of obstacles—appear, that its possessor unwittingly turns propagandist." Another colleague preferred anonymity while declaring that he placed Hall somewhere "in the intellectual twilight zone between genius and insanity. . . ."[24]

Some of his Clark University students, indeed, at times made that institution appear less as a research center than as a center for a new mystic cult led by Hall. "I only touched the hem of [Hall's] . . . garment," recalled one student, "and yet it was a healing touch. I would not give the months I spent at Clark for any other period of my life."[25]

Hall has remained an elusive, enigmatic figure in spite of the long, wide trail he blazed. Repeatedly, just as an understanding of him seems to be within grasp, he mounts a waiting Pegasus and takes flight just beyond reach again. His interpreters have generally attempted to systematize his thought in terms of his puritan heritage or, more broadly, the interplay between himself and thought and action in American society. Hall has been widely accepted as an eclectic, a Puritan, an opportunist, a devotee of individualism, or as a master of Jesuitical casuistry, able to remain "utterly loyal toward one faith and utterly opportunistic toward everything else."[26] Still to be identified, however, is the one faith toward which Hall remained "utterly loyal."

Harvard philosopher Josiah Royce noted in 1919 that Hall, for all his talk of "scientific" truth, was building some strange ideal system. Having read Hall's first major publication, the two-volume *Adolescence* (1904), Royce felt he had read the work of one who thought himself a realist dedicated to scientific truths, but who had unconsciously exposed himself as the owner of "an explicitly idealistic theory." In giving his view of the "real world," wrote Royce, Hall had insisted that a faith in such a world was the only correct, safe, and wholesome doctrine for man. But this world of reality, Royce continued, "being something independent of the minds of us fallible mortals," could be perceived only by Hall. Behind every question about what is real lurked the prior question: What *ought* to be real? "Hence," Royce concluded, "in substance, the real world is such as to embody the ideals of President G. Stanley Hall."[27]

GERMAN IDEALS IN AN AMERICAN EDUCATIONAL STATE

Largely from Darwinian conceptions and Germanic theories of the unconscious mind, Hall developed a "psychonomic law" of recapitulation. According to this "law," all organic matter recapitulated its genetic past in the course of its development. Each individual, therefore, repeated the history of the race as it grew to its present-day level of maturity. Hall noted, however, that institutions and mores of American society, blind to the "law" of recapitulation, twisted, dwarfed, and diverted human organisms from developing according to their innate organic tendencies.

The preadolescent Nordic child, for example, was actually a savage. At that level of maturity he was a living example of early man, a simple creature, barely able to defend himself against other animals. The preadolescent, like the savage, was moved by emotion and will and remained incapable of reasoning. Therefore Hall saw flagrant violations of the true needs of the preadolescent in contemporary educational practices and public expectations of children.

These violations continued at the adolescent level. For although the Nordic youth had moved into a later stage of human development, he still lacked full capacity for reason. He had "thoughtlets." His organic needs took on new forms, but they remained largely physical and emotional. According to Hall, indeed, the present state of "mature" human growth remained for the most part at the adolescent level on the evolutionary scale; most persons who were in years considered adult were actually at the intermediate stage of racial development. Obviously, new educational practices needed to be developed. American institutions had to be reorganized to serve the true needs of man; and new leaders of American society had to be granted the floor.

America stood in deep need of leadership from "genetic psychologists" who could set the nation on the upward evolutionary path again, "on the trail we have so unfortunately lost." Under proper leadership, evolutionary purposes would be served by "the testing of all human institutions by the nature of man and not conversely." Thus, believed Hall, through an Educational State, its programs based on man's true nature and needs, America could serve posterity. Then could the nation prepare for the coming of "collective souls of higher order than our own."[28]

Religious allusions frequently appeared in Hall's essays on education. For Hall, who but for the appeal of Darwin's theory of evolution might have finished his studies at Union Theological Seminary and become a minister, education was "the catholicism, the church universal of to-day."[29] The moral goal of education came through the propagation of a new religion. The "sentiment of reverence, dependence, acquiescence in some great consensus concerning ultimate problems" needed to be inculcated. Seeing soul and mind as inseparable from body, Hall elevated physical culture to the heights of religious duty. The sentiment of reverence, dependence, and acquiescence, nourished in a healthy, hence able, body, was of foremost pedagogical importance;[30] and Hall's goal held far-reaching implications for the "new" school curriculum as well as for teaching methods.

In his praise of physical education Hall early ran afoul of William T. Harris, then Commissioner of the United States Bureau

of Education. While admitting the importance of physical development, Harris stiffly opposed Hall's extreme position; for it chal-
lenged intellectual development as the central aim of schools.
Harris contended that the school must first of all provide tomorrow's men with those materials which *only* a school could provide;
that physical culture should have its place, but outside the school;
that the school in this sense supplemented the home in assuring
the full development of each child.[31] Harris placed himself solidly
behind the existing social structure, behind private property and
accumulations of vast wealth, and from this position acclaimed both
the need for enlightened learning programs and the ability of
American institutions wisely to direct national education and
progress.[32] Hall and Harris were bound to clash. Their mutually
antagonistic ideologies ruffled the decorum of several National
Education Association conferences for nearly thirty years. They
argued, for example, over the question: Do children reason?

HALL: Children do not reason; hence the object of education
is the development of sturdy manhood.

HARRIS: Children do reason.

HALL: Reasoning belongs with higher learning and in particular with the research laboratory.

HARRIS: And do we turn to the laboratory for words of wisdom
about ethics too?[33]

When Hall urged that Latin be dropped from the high school
curriculum, Harris could not suppress a desire to "give three
cheers for Dr. G. Stanley Hall. May he help us to think and see
once in a while how absurd some of his views are!" In reply, Hall
pointedly observed that "men reach an age when the new seems
absurd."[34] More than a verbal dart game was in progress. Harris
worked as a conservator of American education during the rude
transition from agrarianism to industrialism, while Hall spoke for
an elitist minority who admired the German State and longed to
see its facsimile in the land of Jefferson and Jackson.

Behind Hall's denial that children exercised reason loomed his
basic belief that America's faith in reason stood in the way of the
truly Educational State. With Rousseau, however, Hall beheld the
potential for reason as directly proportional to the child's physical
condition. Elementary education, especially, should concentrate
upon physical and emotional growth alone. Critical thinking, as
an aim of education, was the goal of an earlier, unscientific era.
For men should now know, believed Hall, that knowledge—a
powerful, inherently dangerous engine—could enfeeble as well
as strengthen youth. It assuredly strengthened the few—those scientific frontiersmen at the university level who had proven that
their moral and physical strength could direct knowledge into

higher ethical potency for the State. For them alone did knowledge become the path to the private conscience, while for the great mass of mankind a private conscience was "an impractical if not dangerous ideal. . . ."[35] Hall wrote: "For most of us, the best education is that which makes us the best and most obedient servants." Only the "rare moral genius" deserves or even desires a private conscience, because the difficulties in such self-reliance

> are so great that most hasten, more or less consciously and voluntarily, to put themselves under authority again, reserving only the smallest margin of independence in material interests, choice of masters, etc., and yielding to the pleasing and easy illusion that inflates the minimum to seem the maximum of freedom, and uses the noblest ideal of history, viz., that of pure and autonomous oughtness, as a pedestal for idols of selfishness, caprice, and conceit.[36]

Knowledge and personal conscience might be desirable in a democracy whose people must operate under the illusion that the Enlightenment, the Declaration of Independence, and the Constitution bequeathed noble legacies to America. But Hall's "new" Educational State reduced these to adiaphorous virtues at best. Subjects of the "new" regime, for example, would not be confused by being exposed to intellectual problems. Beginning with the lowest grade and continuing throughout the years of formal training, current emphases on intellectual development would be freely replaced by moral training. Wherever intensive study was found, it would be supplanted by extensive study from which generalizations could more readily rush to bolster the didactic purposes of instruction. When teachers finally understood the true aim of education, Hall believed, they would no longer bring disgrace to education by focusing attention upon the average and slower (i.e., less healthy) students; they would appreciate the fact that only the few will be leaders and that the best children in the class must receive the teacher's primary consideration. Slower children should, in fact, be in a "dullard school."[37] Only the few have the "genius and talent" to improve through mental training; meanwhile, they must "set the pace" in the program of physical and emotional development.[38] Indeed, said Hall, it is a question of paramount importance to civilized culture whether mental training, "from the three R's to science and philosophy, shall really make men better, as the theory of popular education assumes."[39]

What will make men better? Hall's answer echoed Plato: Teach men to know and respect their places in the fixed social hierarchy. Dust, polish, and present the glittering myth of the men of gold, silver, brass, and iron. In a paper written for an audience of German educators in 1915, Hall declared that America was the home of men suffering from overstimulation. The myths of the log cabin and rags-to-riches continued to mislead American youth. The presidency and the millionaire were dangled like carrots in front of the dreamily ambitious child. But like the carrot that is never to be eaten, the dream is not to be fulfilled. Overstimulated American children thus become anguished adults, failures in their own eyes, and overcome by the sense of inferiority.[40] An equally dangerous effect of this false stimulation was the implicit emphasis on individualism, always an essential companion to such goads.[41]

HEALTH AND OBEDIENCE IN THE EDUCATIONAL STATE

Most Americans ought to become good servants, said Hall; therefore, teachers must be directed by a new concept of the word "service." Looking upward for inspiration, Hall saw that the "one word now written across the very zenith of the educational skies, high above all others, is the word *service*."[42] The primary and elementary grades, especially, must be permeated with moralizing, physical culture, and the virtues of "habitual and prompt obedience."[43] Moral and religious training, first of all, as the focus of educational endeavor, begins in the cradle. Mother—her face, voice, and nourishment—stands as God to the child. Hall believed that the preschool and kindergarten years, properly utilized, nurtured a gradual expansion of the child's religious sense beyond the mother to nature. No positive instruction in Christian truths, neither moralizing nor clinical discussions, may be given, however. Nor should church-going or public piety be encouraged. Rather, let God remain distant, as he was to primitive man.[44] Let the child know only the Jewish God during preadolescence. The Old Testament stood in Hall's mind as the Bible of youth, supplemented by myths from other sources, both pagan and religious. All stories, indeed, that taught the child to be a faithful servant, rather than a favorite of God, could serve effectively. For preadolescents, who needed practical reasons for righteousness, New Testament altruism was anathema. Few rights should be extended to a child, for he can perform few duties. Invoking his Puritanism to intercede in strengthening the new State, Hall demanded that the "absolute selfishness" of human nature be checked and pruned away, leaving the pure virtue of the subordination of self to authority.[45]

Authority has as its own master, good motives. That authority which supplements good motives will be loved by the child. Hence the child himself, by showing that he loves to be ordered about, will overcome the teacher's possible reluctance to be authoritarian.

As Hall saw it, the child will thus develop "normal, manly independence."[46]

Corporal punishment should never be forbidden. Will-culture "is rarely as thorough as it should be without more or less flogging," wrote Hall. Reverting to psychological and medical similes, Hall prescribed treatment for a child's diseased will. Defiance, disobedience, carelessness, and bravado—the evidences of a diseased will—were likened to a bone which has been set improperly. Just as the doctor, for the good of his patient, rebreaks the limb, so the teacher, for the good of the child (and the State), must likewise break the will. "It is a cruel process," Hall admitted, "but a crampy will in childhood means moral traumatism of some sort in the adult."[47] Obedience should be a law; and the power of corporal punishment as a deterrent to disobedience should be utilized.

> Thus *Dressur* should be the all-pervading aim and method [said Hall]. For essentials or for the staple work of the school which all should be required to take, it should not be necessary to sweeten the decoction much by an appeal to interest, although this, to be sure, has its place. School should be made work and not all play. There should be drudgery, effort, hardness in it, and not too much pleasure or recreation. Again, the teacher should teach with might and main and set the pupils an example of enthusiasm, alertness, and book-work should be reduced to a minimum.[48]

Male teachers in particular are "Olympians," Hall declared, and are able to enforce their will because they own greater strength than children. The good teacher, therefore, should possess the qualities of "a stern disciplinarian, genial withal, but rigorous and relentless in his exactions, and intolerant of all scamped work. . . ."[49]

Effective education as Hall defined it was essentially a question of a healthy body. A child's "animal spirits," he said, were the most reliable clues to his educability. To a gathering at Cooper Union in 1905, Hall made a typical observation: "I almost believe that the boy or girl who has not enough vigor to play a good deal is hardly worth educating at all."[50] Since right actions depend upon a healthy body, will-training efforts are largely wasted upon a body too frail to obey the externally guided mind. And, since mind and muscle are one, body culture is essential to the will-training program. The big muscles, so the Hall argument ran, deserve the larger share of our attention. "The muscles that move the scribbling pen are an insignificant fraction of those in the whole body," Hall discovered, "and those that wag the tongue and adjust the larynx are also few and small."[51] Schools must recognize this verity.

If any school "is in the least degree tending to deteriorate mankind physically," Hall wrote, "it is bad."[52]

Hall put intellectual development in a box and nailed the lid upon it with four pointed arguments for body culture: (1) Body has primacy over mind; only a strong body obeys the servant-oriented mind. (2) American's blind faith in mental training demonstrates that "we have entirely forgotten that men have not only been good citizens but great, who were in idyllic ignorance of even the belauded invention of Cadmus."[53] (3) There are dangers in ideas. Truth itself becomes false and actually immoral in many minds.[54] Even at the high school level, Hall questioned the wisdom of class "discussions" and mock town meetings, for they spawned conceit and a sense of attainment regarding issues about which even the wisest men differed. Hall suspected that the Germans were "right in their insistence upon inculcation, leaving reason and independent judgment and weighing evidence and original investigation to come later" for those who reach a higher, more mature level of attainment.[55] (4) Buoyed by hopes of a coming race of supermen, Hall dreamed of a national program of physical training, one that would not only succeed in improving the race, but that would also lay the foundation for an ultimate, pervasive policy of selective breeding or "stirpiculture." Consequently, the goal of body culture was the superman; and it demanded that youth be induced into "taking an intelligent, serious and life-long interest in their own physical culture and development."[56] According to Hall, "Sooner or later, everything pertaining to education, from the site of the buildings to the contents of every text book, and the methods of each branch of study must be . . . judged from the standpoint of health."[57]

To enact his program Hall advocated an active, intelligent policy of weeding out unfit students at every grade level. Believing that there "are many who ought not to be educated, and who would be better in mind, body, and morals if they knew no school," Hall instructed teachers to ferret out these "many" Platonic men of iron when they were but six- or seven-year-old children. Then, from the group of fit children who were admitted to the schools, he would have the teachers cull the unhealthy (i.e., "slowest") and send them to the aforementioned "dullard school," presumably destined to be men of either brass or iron. From the hardy core that survived these two early raids, several remained who would be able to utilize only the first eight or nine years of school, while a select few would be capable of advancing beyond high school into college and university training. The weeding-out program would continue yearly; and the best students would pass through the grades as rapidly as possible. In his two-volume discussion of *Educational Problems*

Hall even suggested that a three-track (nearly four-track) system in the elementary grades was worthy of consideration.[58]

As a sturdy prop for moral and religious training and body culture, the heart of the "new" education at all levels, Hall employed nature study. While the methods of inculcation and the rest of the curriculum changed as the child moved from elementary to high school, nature study survived the transition, continuing to unlock a world full of object lessons for the child. Awe and reverence fairly filled the child's being when he sat in silent seminar with a grove of trees, or observed flowers, rocks, streams, and felt the immanence of Divinity. Much like Rousseau's Emile, Hall's child learned the practical consequences of understanding nature. The child looked up too. At night he watched "Kant's starry heavens," and by day—a half-hour once or twice each school week—his teacher led him outdoors to study the clouds. He noted their motions, colors, and changes, letting his imagination play among them and his eyes relax from the strain of close work.[59] In the grove as well as in the classroom he sang. Songs of home, nature, "fatherland," and religion drove the finer sentiments into his every fiber.[60] Stories, myths, and great tales calculated to shape his concept of Good had telling effect upon the child's heart.[61] Hall's pantheistic tendencies came into full view in his adulation of nature-study programs. In his allusions to nature study Hall added romantic touches to his more sober views of childlife. Here he made a most native contribution to the religious fervor that greeted the rediscovery of the child at the turn of the century.

With his scheme for the ideal State ever in view, Hall strove vigorously to unite the myriad child-reform agencies under his own leadership. Indeed his child-studies received widespread acclaim from many members of storytelling leagues, big brother and big sister movements, Boy Scouts, mothers' clubs, humane societies, and similar new organizations, all bearing pabulum for the child. Waving the banners of their meliorative crusade, inspired reformers everywhere converged upon infidel desecrators of American youth; and many warriors paused long enough to praise Stanley Hall's inspiration. Hall's *putsch* failed nonetheless. His proposed Children's Institute at Clark University made faltering, futile efforts to achieve unity, order, and a sense of direction from the great coalition of child agencies; it represented his supreme attempt to usurp the religious spark that the rediscovered child had kindled.

SECONDARY SCHOOLING IN THE EDUCATIONAL STATE

In the years before his Children's Institute crumbled in 1911, while Hall laid extensive, if haphazard, plans to revamp education in the United States along the lines of Germany's successes with the Platonic ideal, he was at times optimistic enough to declare that the United States could achieve his goal without adopting centralized government control of education.[62] But Hall could not sustain his hope for the educational millenium under America's existing government structure. Democracy seemed to scoff at Hall's principle, which held that "the one source of vitality in an educational system is *at the top and not the bottom. . . .*" According to him, "every other country in the world to-day save our own" had already turned to centralized government control. He granted that centralization could create dangers for education, but the dangers of our present chaotic system were realities. Simply because Americans had in the past denounced a centralized program as foreign, "we should not forget that in all its best features there is nothing exclusively German, French, English, or Swedish about it. It is a means to an end, and if properly handled would work as well here as so many of our American business forms and inventions have worked when adopted in foreign countries."[63] Even as he argued, however, Hall seemed to realize that the one slender ray of hope for centralization in America came through a crack scarcely wide enough to permit effective ingress to exhortation, casuistry, and literary guerrilla raids upon individualism.

Education for adolescents, meanwhile, received the greatest share of Hall's attention. The elementary program of moral and religious training of course continued in high school, undergoing necessary procedural changes. First of all, as Hall would have it, adolescent boys and girls parted academic company.[64] Separate schools were not necessary, but at the dawn of adolescence boys begin to be men; they need male teachers and a curriculum calculated to prepare them for manhood.[65] Girls, rapidly approaching the age of marriage, need women teachers. Their curriculum—to which Hall paid little more attention than Rousseau paid to Sophie's—was therefore designed to meet their unique needs as future wives and mothers. It did not become a girl to deny her divine procreative task in order that she might become self-sufficient. Women should revel in the glories of womanhood, and should refuse to follow the perverted purposes of feminists who minimized and cast shame upon the sublime goal of womanhood.[66] Hall insisted that his ideal of natural segregation was consistent with social man's history; his ideal had "an immense momentum of history behind it." Declaring that child-study had proven the wisdom of centuries of common practice, he expressed confidence that segregation of the sexes was "not merely custom and tradition, as feminists are wont to assume"; indeed, "the authoritative voice of Nature herself . . . dictates this divergence."[67] Not only did con-

tinued coeducation emasculate young men, but the entire high
school program was thereby becoming feminized. Girls already
outnumbered boys in classes. "If the procession of the last fifteen
years goes on," Hall warned, "our public schools will be dames'
schools."[68]

Separation of the sexes would make possible curricula designed to meet the separate needs of each sex. Boys could then be
instructed in their primary aim of fatherhood and their secondary
aim of employment. Girls would be inspired to fulfill the great commission of motherhood and the soul-shaping of the preschool
child. Both sexes could receive richer instruction in sex hygiene.
Boys and girls would then clearly follow the creed that "parenthood is really the supreme end of man and woman." No longer
would the best physical specimens of American youth ignore their
obligation to posterity. Hall joined Theodore Roosevelt in warning
the nation that the best citizens, by ignoring their procreative obli
gations, were contributing to racial degeneracy. The false ideal of
the medieval monastery and convent, which "left only the worst to
propagate their kind," said Hall, once again threatened to push
mankind backward on the slippery scale of genetic evolution.[69]

The achievement of glorified parenthood required a sustained
attack upon the existing aims of secondary education. Charg-
ing that the high school was "the stronghold of education[al]
conservatism . . . ," Hall worked determinedly to beat down the
false belief in college preparation as a high school function.[70]
Noting that the high school was the chattel of the college when in
reality its adjustment should be to the lower grades, Hall deplored
the high school's mechanical aping of the ways of the college. Fit
only for condemnation were the new edicts from academe that dictated high school curriculum planning in an attempt to tighten the
college's hold on secondary education through a program blindly
designed to give too much education to too many young people.
Above all, Hall dilated upon the need to recognize that high school
training *is* advanced education; that the high school is in reality
the "People's College." The famous 1893 Report of the Committee
of Ten on secondary instruction became a favorite target for Hall's
abuse. Had the Committee recognized the true function of the
high school, its conclusions and recommendations might have
been more "enlightened." When the Committee declared, however, that it was "obviously desirable that the colleges and scientific
schools should be accessible to all boys or girls who have completed
creditably the secondary school course," Hall was certain that
higher education was foisting college entrance requirements upon
high schools in a perverse attempt to expand its student popu-
lations.[71]

In an address before the New England Association of College and High School Teachers in 1902, Hall advocated the counter-organization of a New England Association of Public and English High School Teachers to work independently of the colleges, to fight for an end to college entrance examinations (which made high schools toe the college preparatory line), and to uphold the "democratic" truth that the high school is college for the "people."[72] The high school-college courtship stood as an unholy alliance that undercut the "cultural" aims of Hall's proposed curriculum and substituted a "utilitarian" curriculum built upon the sands of college preparation. "There is need of an organized effort . . . to rescue our high schools from the Philistines of culture," Hall insisted. "These institutions should no longer be content to play an obligato for the college symphony."[73]

If the high school is truly to exist as the home of higher education for the great mass of American children, Hall believed, it must assume responsibility for reviewing the work of the elementary school graduate—just as the college now does for the high school graduate—and if possible remedy the defects of his training thus far.[74] True education begins in adolescence. Now hereditary differences begin to indicate clearly who will achieve a procreant maturity. The years of *Dressur*, will-training, and the Hebraic code can no longer be applied successfully. "We can no longer coerce and break, but must lead and inspire," Hall noted.[75] For those who continue through high school, inspiration becomes the teacher's chief duty. Myths, fables, and storytelling continue, but with a new emphasis. Because adolescence is the age of religious rebirth, the teacher must teach a new orthodoxy. As the child's sentiment deepens and a new self-awareness blossoms forth, the Old Testament's Yahweh ceases to inspire and should therefore be replaced by the altruistic divinity of the New Testament. Perfect religious harmony is thus realized. The Old Testament had taught the child obedience and subservience. Like a broad-axe it had descended upon the child's will and chopped away all defiance, bravado, and selfishness. Now it became the task of the altruistic message of the New Testament to inspire youth with the tender sentiment of service and sublimation of self to the State. "Nothing is so educable as love," Hall said. With proper guidance it "can climb Godward up the stages of a heavenly ladder, as Plato described in the 'Symposium.'"[76]

Hall also remodeled the high school program. There was no room in the reconstructed curriculum for Latin. At a time "when so many other vital studies are clamouring for time and place in the curriculum," Latin's esoteric value was becoming too obscure to permit it to survive.[77] For the great majority of students in the People's College, Latin shamefully wasted human energy. Agreeing heartily with psychologist Edward L. Thorndike, Hall charged that there is no transfer, save in like elements, of power which is trained for efficiency in one direction. "Thus the last stronghold of the apologists of Latin on its present basis is shattered." Properly taught modern languages (German included), on the other hand, received commendation.[78]

Albegra became peeve number two. "It is the most purely formal of all topics"; moreover, it is terribly taught, like Latin. Because algebra is not permitted to grow naturally out of arithmetic, only the most gifted can use it to advantage. For most students it is a "dry, half-meaningless congeries of puzzles and stunts," and therefore rarely useable in later life. The mandate is clear: either teach algebra with a view to its utility in daily life or give it a decent burial along with Latin, the latter undertaking preferred.[79]

With "service" emblazoned "across the very zenith of the educational skies," Citizenship became "the only profession which all young men should be trained for," said Hall. If schools remained so thoroughly laicized as to make the restoration of direct religious training impossible, then civics "must be the new religion of the secular schools."[80] The emerging ideal of brotherhood must therein be captured and fostered as a new secular substitute for the Bibles of the various faiths. The supreme criterion, public service, remained unaffected. All aspects of political procedure must be taught—everything from the electoral college to gerrymandering, and all social issues from immigration to child labor. If American youth are to be expected one day to become voters, continued ignorance about such affairs cannot be permitted to persist.

In expressing this last justification for civics, Hall seemed to be making a great concession to the endurance of America's existing form of government. When related to his views on student participation, however, his program in civics became one of indoctrination. Hall's evolutionary concern for a different tomorrow was instructional in his granting to civics this central position. The spirit of reform filled the air in America. Muckrackers, social gospellers, charity and welfare agencies of all types, educational experimentalists—nearly all who expressed sharp dissatisfaction with the rude turn America had taken while barging into the twentieth century—were welcomed by Hall as potential platoon leaders in a new citizens' army of reconstruction. Beginning in the lower grades and continuing with greater intensity in the high school, patriotism should be taught. The best teacher, perhaps the principal, would define the machinery of ideal national government, teaching "with almost religious, if not pentecostal fervor." The deeds of public heroes ("hero-ology," Hall called it) also belonged to patriotic teachings, because war heroes and military tales helped to save moral instruction from being a "pallid and impoverished thing. . . ."[81]

First, the youth would be inculcated with love of country; second, weaknesses in the existing order would be exposed to him; third, ideal reform measures would be taught. In its bare outline it is the 1-2-3 of successful indoctrination. For Hall's student is the intellectually passive object of rigorous inculcation; he is told what to do, think, and be.

Hall scorned teachers who would "allow or even encourage callow classes to debate, discuss and weigh evidence or regurgitate the matter of the text-book. . . ." Such methods only "flatter the pupils by the subtle suggestion that they can form opinions that merit the name. Instead of exercising power by their crude thoughtlets, *bombinantes in vacuo,* they are inclined to the sweet delusion that their mental emptiness is filled, and so grow complacent with their ignorance, and perhaps opinionated."[82]

English courses had much didactic potential. The English teacher should never concentrate on language or form; rather, he should select materials upon the basis of content and message. Contemporary writers, "whose pages burn with the problems of the present," should be read. All reading, meanwhile, should be rapid, cursory, and extensive. The high school student is not prepared to read intensively and critically. Oratory as the art of influencing conduct with the truth is a part of the English program. So too is drama. An incomparable school of life, plays should be selected on the basis of how well they demonstrate that good is rewarded and evil is punished. Medieval epics are also valuable. Wagner, Shakespeare, Scott, Chaucer, and other writers had found inspiration in knighthood's golden hour. So too should American youth. Chivalry, honor, reverence for womanhood, obedience, justice, heroism—here shimmered a satchel full of the ideals of gentlemen.[83]

Science had as its task to reveal nature as the one great wellspring of all human faith and experience. Students must know and love nature.[84] Therefore physics, which is too drab and unreal, must be deemphasized; and biology, which is closer to life, substituted.[85] Biology opens the door to evolution, instincts, laws of growth in man, physiology, and anthropology—all of which are avenues of expansion closed to physics. In biological studies, Hall maintained, "lie the all-controlling problems of life, health, reproduction, disease, and the place of man in the world, than which nothing is more essential for right living and beside which Latin and even algebra pale in importance, like the moon before the rising sun." Geography, geology, and paleontology, as well as the "genetic aspects" of chemistry should also be surveyed. And, for "a sublime religious sense of awe and reverence so needful and so pregnant for the soul of youth," astronomy should be part of the science curriculum.[86] As for history teaching, Hall said, a greater sense of presentism is absolutely essential. A good text, one which subordinates business, tariff, constitution, and similar topics to the moral aims of history teaching, is needed. Again Hall iterated the need to capture the adolescent's new sense of altruism, of "oughtness," and of duty. The teacher must purify and mint the raw bullion of "humanism" which the adolescent is beginning to reveal. The value of fiction for history teaching should not be ignored. "Much that the modern historian rejects because it happened nowhere is precious because it might have happened anywhere," Hall believed. He proclaimed the myth-building function of history with a blatant frankness reminiscent of Nietzsche. Grimm and Wagner were presented as true historians, as much so as, say, Burkhardt,[87] What a power for moralists lies in the black and white world of didactic fiction, properly selected! "Better in youth, the gushiest, mushiest morass of sentimentality" than the current arid utilitarianism that so controls American schools as to make them "the least morally effective of any on earth."[88]

The last major area of the new curriculum was "muscle" or will-training. Relying heavily upon the virtues of the German gymnastics programs fostered by Guts Muths and Jahn and his Turner Societies, Hall reaffirmed the priority of the body over the mind and of procreation over intellectual development.[89] Accompanying Hall's emphasis on physical culture came industrial training. Besides filling a grave national need, industrial training provided a satisfactory substitute or supplement for military training in the schools. Military training, especially—both in and beyond the last years of school—provided miraculous conditioning powers. Unfortunately, Hall's father had purchased his son's exemption from Civil War service, so Stanley Hall never experienced the joys of which he wrote. He gained only a taste of warfare when he served briefly as a "war correspondent," safely behind the German lines, during the Franco-Prussian War.[90] Nietzsche had at least felt the depersonalizing press of the uniform before a fall from a horse sent him back to civilian life. In both men, however, the Spartan barracks life remained a happy illusion.

> One needs only to glance through a military encyclopedia [wrote Hall] or study Nietzsche to realize the advantages of the aggressive soldierly spirit and attitude. To be chosen by the state, taken away from the home environment, and made to serve the fatherland with a possibility

of offering up life upon one's country's altar gives seriousness, poise, and right orientation, implants not only love of the flag, but *esprit de corps* and regimentation. It abolishes rank and social station and brings a spirit of comradeship, a feeling of good fellowship that may persist through life, and it is believed that now the army is rapidly becoming in all civilized lands a more effective school for personal virtue than ever before.[91]

Military service, said Hall,

gives much advantage of travel and association, and, better yet, young men learn the benefits of discipline, duty, regularity, plain living, habits of hard work, neatness, obedience to authority, a sense of honor, love of the fatherland, better ideas of hygiene. It is, on the whole, a splendid setting-up drill, and those who have had it emerge from this barrack life almost always better in health and morale, with larger intellectual interests, with a quickened sense of loyalty and devotion to the country.[92]

From the perspective of the mid-twentieth century, Hall's educational program and his ecstatic appraisal of the value of military training raise images of the calculated regimen of brown- and black-shirted young men and the brutal power of lock-step cadence that can destroy a bridge or liberty at will. However benign were Hall's educational views before the rise of modern totalitarianism, ideas similar to his gave rise to songs of arrogance and color-splashed processions of uniformed youth, flanked by rows of cheering subjects, and followed by columns of war machines moving serpent-like on caterpillar treads, bent upon fulfilling national destiny at the behest of dictators in Italy and Germany.

With Hall at the helm, the ship of the Educational State took the following general course from kindergarten through high school: Kindergarten and the elementary grades placed heaviest stress upon *Dressur*, fear of the God of wrath, love of country, and body culture. The child thus entered high school with a strong body and a "properly oriented" mind. He became ready to be taught the rewards of service and altruism, having learned well the punishment for selfishness and a "crampy will." Now inspiration supplanted coercion. Patriotism, body culture, and military or industrial education (or both) stimulated and in turn were reinforced by the didactic elements of English, history, and the sciences. Intellectual attainment was widely ignored at all levels. Love of authority, awe of nature, and devotion to State thus transformed the

austere concept of duty into a rewarding sense of personal fulfill-
ment through service to others and the sublimation of self to the
State. Boys and girls, now segregated, were given the great commission to go into all parts of the nation, take unto themselves
healthy mates, and obey posterity's supreme command to pro-
create.

It is little wonder [Lawrence A. Cremin has recently
observed] that for all [Hall's] . . . influence in his own time
he is little celebrated today. Yet it is this very influence that
necessitates our remembering him; for he injected into the
mainstream of American educational thought some of the
most radical—and I happen to think virulent—doctrines of
the twentieth century, and there is no understanding the
present apart from his contribution."[93]

•

CHAPTER FOUR

Atlantis

and the

Great Community

•

Democracy everywhere . . . tends to the dead level of the average man and to the dominance of . . . incompetence and inferiority.

G. STANLEY HALL

Earlier liberalism regarded the separate and competing action of individuals as the means to social well-being as the end. We must reverse the perspective and see that socialized economy is the means of free individual development as the end.

JOHN DEWEY

Only gradually did G. Stanley Hall's perception of the ideal society sharpen. For some years he saw the emerging patterns of German politics as suggesting the kind of state in which the evolving forces of human nature could find expression in higher forms of life. Germany, Hall believed, surpassed all nations in recognizing education as the chief task of statecraft. The land of Plato's *Republic*, which had lain fallow for centuries, was finally being cleared for construction. German science in the late nineteenth century, no longer bound and gagged by institutional Christianity, had already begun to lay foundations. In contemporary Germany, Hall saw the first ivory palaces and streets of gold—his revered Republic in creation. So deeply did Hall admire the educational ideals of Germany that, after nearly six years of study and travel in that country, he longed to live out his days there and foresake America. He even "planned several quite impractical ways of doing so."[1] Immanuel Kant had laid the cornerstone of the Educational State in Germany by freeing science from theology. Encouraged by his contemporaries, the "all-shattering" Kant had stimulated the quest of man for nature's hidden laws by stripping religion bare of superstition, sentimentalism, and moral and theological romanticism. "I have found it necessary to deny God, freedom and immortality," said Kant, "in order to find a place for faith." His philosophy thereby became for many scholars

> the *magna charta* of scientific work. . . . It is a truism to say that among the Germans as nowhere else had developed a positive reverence for science. In what other land does one find in the organic law mention of Science, and read in its constitution an express provision that "Science and its teachings are free"?[2]

Hegel's grand views and the apostolic efforts of Fichte had sketched the dialectic blueprint of the State. The master dialectician's Absolute Idea was embodied in the organic symmetry of the German Educational State. And it was Fichte, Hall believed, who made possible the transformation of the German State concept into a brilliant reality. Fichte's spirit had lived to inspire Germans as they swept away the debris of national disunity. He had especially moved Germans with his stirring cry for a new religion: education. Preaching education as the sole means of drawing man to ultimate perfection, Fichte elevated the scholar to the priesthood. For him education was not only the work of the State, it was also the chief purpose of the State. Ideally, the educator trained, directed, discarded, or elected political leaders, civil servants, artisans—men in the great sweep of occupational fields; and educators at every level stressed morality as the supreme pedagogy and stamped love of the fatherland upon each pupil's breast.

His head filled with Fichte's visions, Hall saw conditions in post-Civil War America that paralleled the rubble of German affairs in Fichte's day. Certainly America was immoral, beset by egotism, ambition, graft, corruption, and a school system tailored to these ends. The Union had been preserved in 1865, but in all important senses to Hall it remained crazy-quilt, blind to the blunder of laissez-faire individualism. American society, as Hall beheld it, testified that internal disorder matched conquest from without as an effective weapon of social destruction. Hall's understanding of the Fichtean program convinced him that its general outlines pointed out America's way to salvation. Even when Fichte turned his thoughts toward a later State socialism Hall was momentarily tempted to follow. Hall's studies of genetics, psychology, evolution, and Plato, however, turned him back to a State concept in which every man knew his place in a class hierarchy based upon principles of human inequality and in accordance with the laws of heredity and evolution.

Hall admired the Germanic stress on the moral end of education. Learning must harmonize with the greater morality of the state rather than of the individual; it must truly promulgate the concept of public service and sublimation of self to the State. Educational emphases, therefore, must be shifted from attention to the development of the intellectual capacities (for personal development) to make way for the primacy of physical culture (for the service of the State). If men are to serve, they must be *able* to serve; they must learn to be servants. The implication is obvious. Hall's syllogism thus began to run counter to that of Fichte, Harris, and others who placed emphasis upon intellectual attainment; it was in closer harmony with the Platonic State concept and paid due tribute to the priority of the Unconscious over the Conscious. Herbert Spencer had here performed a crucial abstract stunt for Hall's purposes: First, he elevated matter to a high union with mind, then he deftly transmuted mind into matter, thereby contributing scientific corroboration of Rousseau's advocacy of physical culture and intuition. Eduard Von Hartmann's philosophy of the Unconscious and Sigmund Freud's controversial investigations in the world of the Subconscious further stimulated Hall's skepticism about human reason.[3]

When teachers poured knowledge into a child's mind, Hall believed they spread the germs of an enervating disease. Knowledge sapped man's vitality by leading him to ignore his physical development; it spawned seeds of doubt where certainty should grow; it destroyed man's usefulness to the State by giving unwarranted elevation to his ego. Knowledge was dangerous, in short. Instead, said Hall, evolutionary truths lead one to conclude that most men should be given only the Noble Lie, myths, and gymnastics. His words sent a new breeze rustling through Plato's Academy.

Next to be incorporated as part of Hall's system were the robust idealisms of Schopenhauer and Nietzsche. The creation of the superman—*the uebermensch*—became the crowning aspiration of Hall's ideal State. But the idea of the superman soon created a system-building problem for Hall. Frankly captured by the power of Nietzsche's expression, Hall wavered for a time toward the egoistic description of the superman, only to realize that he thereby undermined his entire system by appropriating an *uebermensch* whose personality made him unfit to guide and inspire a State dedicated to harmony, accord, and service. To sterilize those subjects who possessed undesirable traits and scientifically to mate and breed healthy subjects was certainly consistent with the Good. However, if service and altruism were to be the ideals of the evolutionary state, then the superman must be the perfect physical embodiment of these ideals. Not until Germany fell in 1918 did Hall completely cast aside the Nietzschean superman and begin fully to appreciate the need for consistency at the lofty apex of his State. Only then did Hall sketch the image of a different superman on the *tabula rasa* of the future. His final strokes revealed a mortal, muscular Jesus.[4]

With few such modifications of the Teutonic prototype, Hall's plans called for a new America that would mirror the new Germany. Upon his return to the United States in 1880 from his second extended visit of Germany, however, Hall "felt the whole atmosphere of this country and especially of staid old New England, most oppressive and not only unappreciative of about all I most cared for but distinctly critical if not derisive of the new views, tastes, and *mores* which I brought back."[5] On the one hand, the German State continued to tantalize him with the possibility that his scheme might succeed in America. On the other hand, because he dreaded personal controversies and clashes, his desire to speak up for his ideals was repeatedly frustrated. His greatest conscious fears sprang from contemplating the necessary antagonisms his words would create, the inevitable clash with leadership and its vested interest in gilded age America, and the possible overestimation of his own qualifications for the role of prophet. He felt temperamentally inadequate to rush into action and to put his ideas to the test of open combat. While he dreamed of greatness, of preaching the philosophical gospel of America's future before a nation of believers, he lacked the zeal to follow his star openly. More than anything else Hall dreaded "every form of conflict and disharmony," a dread which he felt came to him from his mother's almost masochistic devotion to Puritanism's God. Hall confessed in later life:

> Any marked disagreement with those nearest me is often paralyzing. If I am not assured of sympathy in my social environment it is hard for me to speak or to assert myself. . . . Thus there is an inveterate dislike of the open, a dread of being conspicuous, a love of obscurity, of the simple private life, of homely commonplace people, that has kept me in touch with the rural friends of my boyhood.[6]

His idealism, however, would not remain sublimated. It came to light—piecemeal, to be sure—as a paragraph in an article here or a point in a speech there. Hall inched his program for the Educational State forward a tentative step at a time, never really sure whether the response he won signaled warm support, icy indifference, or imminent danger. He never delivered a series of evangelical Fichtean addresses to the American nation. In America Hall cautiously set for himself the tremendous problem of establishing a strong and inspired educational system with which to reconstruct the nation itself. Despite the poor odds, the idea of progress toward the Educational State was too necessary, too noble, in Hall's mind, to permit its suppression. Hall was to become the piecemeal prophet.

I

HALL IN ADVOCACY OF THE EDUCATIONAL STATE

In 1881, before members of the American Social Science Association, Hall delivered one of his earliest sympathetic resumes of Fichte's plan for the Educational State. Praising the results of this plan as "the very best products of civilization in Germany," Hall further insisted that Germany's national and material strength had its source in the waters of a pure pool from which all nations could drink. From the Fichtean fount, said Hall, a refreshed Germany had risen to overcome immense problems; she learned to pay allegiance to

> the lofty ministry of education. . . . More than any other government she has known how to adopt the best features of both the Roman and Greek states. . . . [Moreover, Germany, in the best sense of the idea, had] actualized the Platonic Republic, in which the chief care of the lawgiver was the education of the young. Her methods and aims in this direction are now, especially since the Franco-Prussian War, slowly gaining force in the school legislation of most countries of continental Europe, as well as, [Hall hopefully added] in our own.[7]

Whether a republican form of government can endure, Hall said, is basically a question of the truistic need for education. Stating flatly that "John Stuart Mill is wrong"—that Mill's notion of freedom worked to the detriment of both school and nation—Hall asserted that the "*laissez-faire, laissez-aller* principle is suicidal in a republic—impressive as is the casuistry with which it is so often defended. There must be despotism here if need be." Education must be made mandatory; every device from coaxing to flogging must be employed to make Hall's program effective, to drive out "lower selfish motives" and implant the high motives which give birth to "Moral Freedom." Germany recognized that moral training *is* education; she had achieved this equation largely because she wisely refused to separate church and state. Admitting that Americans preferred this rupture, Hall nonetheless insisted that the separation never was, is, or will be absolute; and "it must not be too rigorously insisted upon."[8]

Hall repeatedly contrasted the dark immorality of the "old" education—with its mechanistic, complacent routine—against the true moral brilliance of the "new" education he would import. The current school system, "better adapted to educate henchmen of political and other bosses," lacked both internal guidance and a sense of national direction—the very qualities that buoyed the German system. Americans must realize what German education "has brought in military success and supremacy, and is now giving in increased industrial leadership"; then they would understand that the United States must make education its "duty of duties." America too, Hall demanded, "must realize the platonic republic where the wisest ruled and education was the chief problem of statesmanship. This policy must be our destiny. Our leaders must be the priests of Truth and in her pay."[9]

America respected the utility of system, Hall believed, but delusions about the sanctity of individualism had given the nation a weak body for an otherwise healthy mind. System implies arrangement, ordering, and the creation of a necessary hierarchy of values or procedures. Thus Hall doubted that America, recognizing these implications, would soon accept the Educational State; America's faith held that government must be weak, despite the rampages of ragged individualism and the exploitation of resources. Nevertheless, the one source of vitality in an Educational State rested at the top, not the bottom—and system was the secret of vitality. The national need for thought-conversion encouraged Hall to continue to preach the glories of his "new" education, even though many of his ideas were tossed about like indignant chips on the rising waters of meliorism and empiricism in American education.[10]

G. Stanley Hall thus exulted in the spirit of morale generated by Americans during World War I. Willing self-subordination and unquestioning service to goals visible only to great public leaders, so essential to social harmony, had come to America! With the return of peace, morale needed only to be sustained and bent to the service of the Educational State and the quest for supermanhood.

Hall viewed 1919 as a critical year. Which way would Americans turn? Would men take the upward path of genetic psychology or would degenerative tendencies, already at work, force mankind to slide back toward the chaos of the gilded age? Americans needed to be warned, perhaps by a utopian tale that illustrated the psychological principles of true human progress. During the summer of that year Hall set for himself a reading program in utopian novels. In 1920 he wrote his own story of the Good Society, "The Fall of Atlantis."[11]

ATLANTIS

In its days of glory Atlantis, as Hall depicted it, was the perfect Educational State. At its apex university research scholars guided social destiny and conducted experiments in selective breeding for supermen. At other levels of learning "heart-formers" supervised the process of drawing children through the steps of human growth. Health, stamina, the capacity for play, service, and procreativity were the criteria for educability.[12]

"Heart-formers," the psychologists in Atlantis, also guided the nation's religious life. They offered courses in fetishisms, totemisms, nature-worship, and cults of every kind. Each student could choose any cult that suited his emotional sense of reality or reject them all, "realizing that all were only symbols, incarnations, or guides" to an appreciation of the mystic process of evolution. Those who had evolved farther along the genetic scale turned to anthropomorphism for their spiritual needs, while others less advanced chose more primitive cults with perfect freedom and without shame or resentment. "Practically men were accounted religious in Atlantis if they were truly altruistic and not predominantly self-seeking, and all here were taught to die cheerfully, contemplating the good they had done."[13]

Moral problems of business, sex education, mental health, and marriage problems also came under the eye of the "heart-formers." They concentrated, however, upon the sex education of pubescents and adolescents. Male "heart-formers" took the boys and female "heart-formers" led the girls through the "sacred mysteries of sex." It was the high obligation of the Atlantean psychologist to convince youth that "the responsibility to transmit the holy torch of life undimmed to the innumerable unborn was . . . the chief end of life."[14] With this point made clear, the "heart-formers" later arranged matings for marriage and procreation.

But in the midst of this Atlantean splendor, so strongly reminiscent of Plato's Cretan city of *The Laws*, degenerative forces began to work. Hall showed how egotism, cries for "*my* rights," and labor agitation in Atlantis destroyed altruism, the sense of duty, and social harmony based on a hierarchy of classes. Let this be a warning to Americans, "for we can still hearten ourselves against relapse by the warnings that have now most opportunely come to us from out of the depths of the sea."[15]

Hall made it as clear in "Atlantis" as in his professional writings that, for him, man was most noble and valuable when he served posterity. Man was not the measure; nor was some eternal, unchanging Good. The ever-evolving need of posterity was the measure of all things. Yet individual man had a kind of immortality, obtainable through reproduction. Man became a link in the unbroken chain of evolution. Standing on the shoulders of earlier life-forms, man lifted his offspring ever closer to supermanhood.

Hall's Educational State, as it peered through his professional writings and blossomed in "Atlantis," turned early nineteenth-century social reconstructionism on its head. Maclure and the Owens had claimed that science revealed man's nature to be plastic, his mind a blank and ready for simple facts at birth, with reason the controlling factor in his growth and behavior. Hall claimed that science revealed man's nature to be fixed by the experiences of his racial forebears, his mind a small inchoate muscle, and his will and emotion the determinants of his conduct. Heredity supplanted environment in the Educational State.

In the new nation men like Maclure and the Owens had sought freedom from ignorance and from an indoctrination for human subservience which they saw as the shared aim of church and state. The Educational State was to have been achieved through microcosmic reform in America. Community-by-community regeneration obviated any opportunity for a strong central government or national church to gain control of national education. Hall reinstated both church and state in a macrocosmic plan of regeneration.

Against those Educational States dedicated to promote human rights and reason, Hall raised a State premised on human duty and emotion. While many former States had nurtured self-interest as the root of social harmony, Hall's State exorcised the demon of self-interest and proclaimed altruism the motor of man's highest morality. The early nineteenth-century social reconstructionists had sought to provide the means for securing man's humanity to man; Hall established an Educational State dedicated to the proposition that humanity had been created to serve super-humanity. No longer heeded was the outworn dictum: "Control nature that it may better serve man's noble purposes." In its place appeared the new slogan: "Control man that he may better serve nature's noble purposes."

Granville Stanley Hall turned paternal primitivist. Invoking Plato, Darwin, and Freud, he warned Americans that modern society must abandon any quest for greatness based upon faith in individual reason and merit.

II

JOHN DEWEY AND THE GREAT COMMUNITY

When the "Fall of Atlantis" was written, Hall's old protagonist Harris no longer led the opposition. A new voice, that of John Dewey, now held the ears of American educators. Dewey's earliest philosophical romance had been with the work of Hegel, the same work that had guided William T. Harris throughout his career, and as a graduate student at the Johns Hopkins University Dewey had studied psychology under G. Stanley Hall. In those days the discipline of psychology had not been detached from that of philosophy, and Dewey's earliest writings were on subjects later to be identified with psychology.

Soon Dewey was to reject all transcendental teleology, all cosmic purposing, that of Harris' pure spirit as well as that of Hall's evolutionary human instincts. Hall dismayed Dewey by fostering the debilitating notion that "the world must be approached from the animistic standpoint."[16]

For radically different reasons John Dewey shared some of Hall's disappointment with the conditions and purposes of modern American life. But while Hall turned to the ideological right, Dewey moved to the left. Nor could Dewey concur with William T. Harris who beheld America's budding Great Society and called it Good. Dewey demurred, "The Great Society created by steam and electricity may be a society but it is no community."[17] The effects of exploitive technology and uncontrolled demographic trends were patently destructive elements of the so-called Great Society. "The invasion of the community by the new and relatively impersonal and mechanical modes of combined human behavior is the outstanding fact of modern life."[18]

The central facts of the human condition remained mysteries when Hegel laid the rules for inquiry. Dewey, having come through the Hegelian ranks himself, was forced to conclude that a faith in State, in the teleological necessities of the onward-and-upward dialectic, destroyed the idea of progress as the fruit of social initiative and purpose. To paraphrase Kant, Dewey found it necessary to deny the Doctrine of Progress in order to admit that progress could be made. An acceptance of the Doctrine exposed one to a pernicious immobilization.

The idea of cosmic Progress, breathing optimistic life into all human relationships, encourages one to believe that the present is inferior to the future, *but* that necessarily small, evolutionary steps are currently being taken to insure a better tomorrow. Hence, one becomes the patient liberal, the soothing voice of sympathy and hope, the secular minister who delivers kindly messages and an occasional basket of bread to the Have-Not. Mix this Enlightenment notion with the upward march of Hegelian thought and the activities of the patient liberal become scarcely distinguishable from the cautious conservative.

With a generation of intellectuals bred in the atmosphere of small towns of nineteenth-century America and forced in their mature years to wrestle with axiological problems in the impersonal and mechanical blindness of mushrooming megalopoli, Dewey developed a lasting respect for the earlier more intimate method of human intercourse peculiar to rural and small-town America. A restoration of the "face-to-face community," but not of small-town society itself, became for him the life-blood of heightened social attainment and individual dignity, of truly "progressive" change, and of the necessary development of the idea of democracy from its beginnings as a political device to a way of living that embraced equalitarian treatment of man and purposive collective action in all human affairs. Whether he spoke of domestic national life or, as in the following statement, of international relations, his point was the same: "The only way to make headway is to start with the nonpolitical aspects of society—conversation, food, technical meetings, congresses and so on—and end up with politics. But certainly don't start with politics!"[19] On the occasion of his ninetieth birthday the same line of thought, now a fixed aim in Dewey's mind, reappeared: "Democracy begins in conversation."[20]

Jefferson, even Maclure, and William James suggested human goals and methods that became more worthy of support for Dewey than did those proposed by Harris or Hall. None of the former exalted the State over the citizen or failed to support the idea that man, whose nature was plastic, could become a reasoning creature. Education was not a "system of police" to use Daniel Webster's phrase; it was a force of liberation for man. Not to be confused with mere "schooling," education was for Dewey a lifelong experience. Ideally it developed habits of suspended belief, inquiry, and the willingness to change, by reasoned choice, any and all institutionalized forms of life in response to keener insights about the conditions necessary for the continued elevation of the quality of life. Here was the educational desideratum, then: to involve all members of society in processes meliorative for the human spirit.

By the time Dewey established his experimental school at the University of Chicago (1896) he had adopted a view of progress not unlike that earlier espoused by William Maclure. That is to say, he saw the drive for property, knowledge, and social control as fundamental. Changes in technology that he recognized as evidences of the increased scientific attitude on the part of man, had, he believed, outrun changes in other human institutions. Evil was a function of man's failure to use creative intelligence with respect to these other institutions. Cultural lag, the failure to study and adjust all institutions along with the reorganization of technology, was the source of most problems.

Social disorganization was anathema to Dewey as to Harris and Hall; social order and harmony among men was prized by Dewey as by them. But to him neither the evolutionary outworking of the world soul nor the biological evolution of human instincts could be relied upon to provide this order. What was needed was the deliberate use of cooperative human intelligence, fortified by a scientific attitude and focused upon the relations among social institutions. With the political progressives of his day Dewey saw social reform as a matter of human engineering, with efficiency tempered by humaneness the criteria for success. Though he rejected the state as the embodiment of human virtues and aspirations, he came very close to putting the "community" in its place.

Developments in technology, he argued in *School and Society* (1899), had robbed the family and the village shop of their capacity to aid the young in seeing life whole and integrated. Work had lost its significance, which is to say that one no longer saw intimate relationships between his function as a producer and as a member of a group sharing affection, mutual respect, and common purpose. Academic instruction and scientific inquiry were also now cut off from a direct and immediate connection with the problems and aspirations of men. The pedagogical answer was to re-establish in the school a miniature, embryonic community. By engaging the young in cooperative problem solving, oriented initially around relatively primitive processes of production but following the history of these processes to the contemporary complex level, one could hopefully sharpen a sense of the connectedness and interdependence of modern life and thought.

In *The Child and the Curriculum*, a companion volume to *School and Society*, Dewey addressed himself to the Rousseauvian concern with self-realization. Passages abound in which he waxed eloquent about the case for the child: "The case is of the Child. It is his present powers which are to assert themselves; his present capacities which are to be exercised; his present attitudes which are to be realized."[21] But he was far from Rousseauvian in his criteria about the ultimate image in which child growth should be shaped.

According to *The Child and the Curriculum*, the teacher's sense of the most scientific and efficient ways in which the race has so far developed for responding to problems is crucial in providing direction. Where the experience of the race is not controlling, one's contribution to the group endeavor proves critical. What function a particular child has in a group project will reflect his highly personal interests and capacities, but whether or not it is worthwhile is judged by its value to the common enterprise. The sense of community, which Dewey was most concerned to establish, depended on each child accepting the group's aspiration as his own and allocating esteem to himself and to his peers in terms of service to these aspirations. Of course it was fundamental to Dewey's scheme that the group be "democratic," that all participate in determining what projects are undertaken.

This early Dewey saw changes in the processes for producing and distributing goods and services in the forefront of social change generally. At a time when he momentarily toyed with the recapitulation theory as the possible explanation of this economic evolution, he saw the study of these processes as the most promising clue to organizing instruction. Also at this time one can see emerging something of a Marx-Bellamy orientation; and Dewey himself once suggested that Marx's *Das Kapital* and Bellamy's *Looking Backward* were among the books most markedly shaping his convictions. But Dewey was certainly not at this time a radical social reformer. Nothing in these early proposals need have threatened those in power. Dewey hoped such schools as his would evolve active, productive citizens who would be concerned about social situations, but his was no school for rebels. There is in the early Dewey no call for fundamental assaults on private ownership, nor is there any of the Freudian notion that the basic impulses and desires of the individual might directly clash with institutional social interests.

During the 1920's Dewey's public views began to change. Though later disillusioned with the Soviet experiment, Dewey saw in the revolutionary movements of the twenties new possibilities in the fundamental reforms of political and economic institutions. In that decade he traveled widely—to Russia, Turkey, Mexico, and China. Citizens and government leaders alike stirred Dewey with their enthusiastic, even passionate, efforts to build greater communities in their lands. In Russia, for example, he found the identification of formal education with political propagandizing repugnant; but he also found that "The main effort is nobly heroic, evincing a faith in human nature which is democratic beyond the ambitions of the democracies of the past."[22]

> Much of what he found in Leninist Russia therefore
> came as a shock. In view of the prevailing idea of other coun-
> tries as to the total lack of freedom and total disregard of
> democratic methods in Bolshevist Russia, it is disconcerting,
> to say the least, to find Russian school children much more
> democratically organized than our own; and to note that
> they are receiving . . . a training that fits them, much more
> systematically than is attempted in our professedly demo-
> cratic country, for later active participation in the self-
> direction of both local communities and industries.

Indeed Dewey found in the budding school system of Leninist
Russia ideas "from which we might, if we would, learn much more
than from the system of any other country."[23]

No clearer illustration of the ideological distance between
Dewey and Hall could be found than in their discussions of "democracy" in the United States and in Russia. "Democracy *everywhere* . . . ," Hall insisted, "tends to the dead level of the average
man [whose abilities are sorely limited by heredity], and to the
dominance of . . . incompetence and inferiority."[24]

And what of Leninist Russia in Hall's estimation? Hall admitted certain virtues of the new regime; but after weighing them
against their accompanying fallacies, he concluded that Bolshevism
was "democratization gone mad." It had become a wounded Poly-
phemus, stumbling in blind pursuit of a classless society. There
must be classes in any society, Hall argued. Russia's chances for a
successful venture therefore depended upon "The ability of the
soviet leaders to organize upward till each class has its proper
place."[25] Her leaders must therefore open their eyes to another
important maxim: "If the wealth of any land were equally divided,
everybody would be poor, not rich."[26] Religion too must be cher-
ished as an asset rather than ostracized as a threat to the State.
Selfishness, which Hall saw in evidence at the higher echelons of
Russian government, must be obliterated and service and brotherhood be instated.[27] Thus, by abstract tinkering—here discarding a
cog, there adjusting a bolt and changing the firing order—Hall
tuned up the Bolshevik engine. When he had finished, the engine
hummed much like his own ideal State.

Dewey, however, set himself against the authoritarian state
ideal and against the social ignorance that permitted changes to
proceed in unforeseen, uncontrolled directions. Desperately
needed, then, was the creation of responsible channels for change.
Opposed to the elitism so dear to Hall, Dewey sought a social order
committed to an equality of concern for all its members and to
faith in human potential.

Clearly not a "belly liberal"—one who fights for material security *per se*—Dewey charged that

> To "make others happy" except through liberating their powers and engaging them in activities that enlarge the meaning of life is to harm them and to indulge ourselves under cover of exercising a special virtue. Our moral measure for estimating any existing arrangement or any proposed reform is its effect upon impulse and habits. Does it liberate or suppress, ossify or render flexible, divide or unify interests? Is perception quickened or dulled? . . . Is thought creative or pushed one side into pedantic specialisms? There is a sense in which to set up social welfare *as an end* of action only promotes an offensive condescension, a harsh interference, or an oleaginous display of complacent kindliness. [But to] foster conditions that widen the horizon of others and give them command of their own powers, so that they can find their own happiness in their own fashion, is the way of social action. Otherwise the prayer of a freeman would be to be left alone, and to be delivered, above all, from "reformers" and "kind" people.[28]

Russia seemed to Dewey to have learned "the way of social action." Not democratization gone mad, but democracy of heroic potential proportions greeted Dewey. The schools and communities supported one another in shaping an enriching life of culture and a shared joy of learning and working together.

> Perhaps the most significant thing in Russia, after all, is not the effort at economic transformation, but the will to use an economic change as the means of developing a popular cultivation, especially an esthetic one, such as the world has never known. [And again,] . . . the final significance of what is taking place in Russia [in the 1920's] is not to be grasped in political or economic terms, but is found in change, of incalculable importance, in the mental and moral disposition of a people, an educational transformation. This impression, I fear, deviates widely from the belief of both the devotees and the enemies of the Bolshevik régime. But it is stamped in my mind and I must record it for what it is.

Refreshing too, and enlightened, was the freedom from race and color prejudice that seemed to lend reassuring credence to the plan to bring *all* persons into the cultivated life. Nor was Dewey insensitive to the Russian charge that " . . . a nation that strives for a private culture from which many are excluded by economic stress cannot be a cultivated nation. . . . . "[29]

Driven with renewed purpose to explore the obstacles standing between divided Americans and an inheritance of generous union and face-to-face community encounter, Dewey thus severed the democratic spirit from any necessary connection with capitalism.[30] Dewey pondered, "I do not see how any honest educational reformer in western countries can deny that the greatest practical obstacle in the way of introducing into schools that connection with social life which he regards as desirable is the great part played by personal competition and desire for private profit in our economic life." Here was Dewey, who for a generation had been identified with the idea of the school as an integral and integrating institution in the community, now leading himself to the logical conclusion that such interrelationships under capitalism sabotaged the higher purposes of educational reform. He accepted the conclusion in its general form; and continued by noting that the socioeconomic fact of American life "almost makes it necessary that *in important respects school activities should be protected from social contacts and connection, instead of being organized to create them.*" If that were not clear enough, Dewey spelled out the meaning of honest educational reform with unmistakeable clarity, at the same time reaffirming his earlier stress on community values: "The Russian educational situation is enough to convert one to the idea that *only in a society based upon the cooperative principle can* the ideals of educational reformers be adequately carried into operation."[31] In the Russia of the 1920's, at least, intellectuals and educational reformers seemed to be building a potentially enviable community ideal with the power thrust of "a unified religious social faith." What, then, was now the role of honest intellectuals in America? In America intellectuals "have a task that is, if they are sincere, chiefly critical. . . ."[32]

In a sober "Critique of American Civilization," prepared at the request of the Chautauqua in 1928, Dewey resisted prophecy in favor of query and criticism.

> Where are we going? Toward what are we moving? . . . If ever there was a house of civilization divided within itself and against itself, it is ours today. If one were to take only some symptoms and ignore others, one might make either a gloomy or a glowing report, and each with equal justice—as far as each went.

The public and official elements of American life, typified by a general "hardness, a tightness, a clamping down of the lid, a regimentation and standardization, a devotion to efficiency and prosperity of a mechanical and quantitative sort," filled Dewey with "discouragement." But in the ferment on the fringe of what has since been labeled the "Establishment" he took heart. To the "outside" and private circles—focussing upon scattered leaders of the intelligentsia—Dewey looked expectantly for men to write a slogan more noble than "Prosperity is our God." Hopefully the potential cultural dynamism of the private sector would organize its aimless patterns of protest (and bohemianism) into a relevant statement of individual potential and worth. "In saying this," Dewey added, "I do not mean what is sometimes called individualism as opposed to association. I mean rather an individuality that operates in and through voluntary associations."[33] Dismayed by the lethal lethargy of the public sector Dewey saw the main hope for reform in a grass roots impulse of unified private groups. Thus his own energies poured as a testimony to his own action-oriented philosophy. He either attended the birth or encouraged the development of several organizations including the National Association for the Advancement of Colored People, the American Association of University Professors, the American Federation of Teachers, and the League for Industrial Democracy.

All this had taken place before the depression of the 1930's. During that decade, with a nation strife-wracked and simmering with social desperation, Dewey made his sharpest attacks upon economic competiton. *Carpe diem.* Let the ideal of shared human purpose, of universalized culture, of man dignified now guide the national effort to pull free of the muck of widespread misery. Now, he insisted, reverse the traditional relationship between man and economic machinery. Let technology and production no longer dictate human purpose; but let them now be bent to the task of liberating man from the curse of exploitation and economic competition.

> The actual corrosive "materialism" of our times [Dewey insisted in 1935] does not proceed from science. It springs from the notion, sedulously cultivated by the class in power, that the creative capacities of individuals can be evoked and developed only in a struggle for material possession and material gain. We either should surrender our professed belief in the supremacy of ideal and spiritual values and accommodate our beliefs to the predominant material orientation, or we should through organized endeavor institute the socialized economy of material security and plenty that will release human energy for pursuit of higher values. . . . Regimentation of material and mechanical forces is the only way by which the mass of individuals can be released from regimentation and consequent suppression of their cultural

possibilities. . . . Earlier liberalism regarded the separate
and competing action of individuals as the means to social
well-being as the end. We must reverse the perspective and
see that socialized economy is the means of free individual
development as the end.[34]

Where in all this macrocosmic planning did the schools of
America fit? To the consternation of social reconstructionists of
the 1930's, Dewey refused to support their desire to make the
schools a center for propagandizing the virtues of the anticipated
socialized commonwealth. He continued to insist upon the essentially undemocratic nature of indoctrination. It would be enough—
even more than too many teachers were capable of—to focus upon
intellectual freedom and thorough understanding of the salient
facts of historical and contemporary society.

To be free an individual had to be at liberty to choose between
alternatives fairly presented. The idea of indoctrination, however
innocuously pushed by some social reconstructionists, bode fair to
threaten the principle of choice. Freedom of inquiry amounted to
social inquiry. All studies should be taught according to the principle that the basis of correlation is social life. Thus too, Dewey explicitly charged the schools with a task that consciously refused to
build any fixed social ideal for American youths; schools were to
vest in youth the freedom and ability to modify their institutions
according to their own best sense of community in the coming day
of their own maturity. Dewey recognized and heartily endorsed a
twentieth-century version of Jeffersonian enthusiasm for viewing
societies as experiments in living.

Many powerful interest groups, however, consciously restrained freedom of inquiry. They recognized, Dewey maintained,
that if teaching "starts with questions and inquiries it is fatal to all
social system-making and programs of fixed ends. . . . It is not easy
to imagine the difference which would follow from the shift of
thought to discrimination and analysis."[35] A democratic public
required clearly more than mere freedom of inquiry. Free dissemination of the conclusions of inquiry, free debate, full discussion,
and intelligent and intellectually honest persuasion were also essential. Too long had men been led to believe that to be free in
one's thought was tantamount to fulfilling the meaning of free
inquiry. Mind is not severed from action. Such a notion "presents
in fact the spectacle of mind deprived of its normal functioning,
because it is baffled by . . . actualities . . . and is driven back into
secluded and impotent revery."[36]

The school, then, should foster freedom of expression. Without that successful effort, social inquiry remained an idle fantasy.

Freedom to inquire, to express opinions and render reasoned judgments with impugnity, to combat the oligarchical interests that encouraged social inertia, prejudice, and blind emotion in the interests of mass manipulation—these purposes should guide the efforts of schoolmen. Then all knowledge, unified and directed at social purposes, would make intelligence a community property. "A fact of community life which is not spread abroad so as to be a common possession is a contradiction in terms. . . . Communication of the results of social inquiry is the same thing as the formation of public opinion."[37] A perpetrated lie can thus be *public* opinion in name alone.

But this was far from asserting that the child should dictate his own course of study and activity. Dewey attacked the sentimental and the psycho-analytical advocates of child-centeredness as "stupid." Those who with Harris would be content simply to set the child to memorize lessons in "subject-centered" programs also missed the Deweyan pedagogical point. As Arthur Wirth observed in his provocative study of *John Dewey as Educator*, Dewey

> resisted an either/or choice between values that cluster about "individuality" and those that center about "community." . . . The uniqueness of the *individual* accounts for values like creativity, challenge, and innovation. Yet the individual is not truly human without the nourishment of community. Unchecked, his freedom can degenerate into self-indulgence, exhibitionism, or anarchistic iconoclasm. *Community* is the source of fellowship, solidarity, hard-won knowledge and supportive traditions. But compulsive concern with these can bring conformity, coercion, and stagnation.[38]

It was Dewey's attempt, one he recognized as "The ultimate problem of all education," to maintain the imperative but fragile balance between "permissiveness" and "other-directedness."[39]

Ceaseless striving for balance of these interests implied the presence of "democratic methods" in all human relationships. For wherever democracy had failed it had been conceived as

> too exclusively political in nature. It had not become part of the bone and blood of the people in daily conduct. . . . Democratic forms were limited to Parliament, elections and combats between parties. What is happening [in the 1930's] proves conclusively, I think, that unless democratic habits of thought and action are part of the fiber of a people, political democracy is insecure.[40]

But schools failed abysmally wherever their interests in democratic processes found primary expression in student government, bland meandering classroom discussions calculated merely to let each child "have his say," and didactic exercises in social courtesy. Respect for purpose, intelligence, and habits of inquiry had to be sedulously cultivated. How, for example, could schools claim to be preparing youth "for any kind of democratic self-government," Dewey pondered, when schoolmen lacked the courage or knowledge to teach the realities of modern governmental operations? Knowledge of government, as taught when Dewey wrote this critique in 1937, was not

> much connected with how government is actually run, with how parties are formed and managed, what machines are, what gives machines and political bosses their power. In fact, it might be dangerous in some cities if pupils in the schools were given not merely a formal and anatomical knowledge about the structure of the government but also acquired an understanding of how the government of their own community is run through giving special favors and through dealings with industrial powers.[41]

With this example of Dewey's concern for relating an ideal to the actual, one might suspect that he would also require the teacher to align himself with social reconstruction in the interests of widening the democratic tradition. Unwilling to be misunderstood on this crucial point, Dewey spoke of the teacher's position as similar to Hamlet's. The teacher who knew that

> the times are out of joint [could not escape] some responsibility for a share in putting them right. . . . Drifting is merely a cowardly mode of choice. I am not trying here to tell teachers with which of the antagonistic tendencies of our own time they should align themselves—although I have my own conviction on that subject. I am trying only to point out that the conflict is here, and that as a matter of fact [teachers] . . . are strengthening one set of forces or the other. *The question is whether they are doing so blindly, evasively, or intelligently and courageously.* If a teacher is conservative and wishes to throw in his lot with forces that seem to me reactionary and that will in the end, from my point of view, increase present chaos, *at all events let him do it intelligently, after a study of the situation and a conscious choice made on the basis of intelligent study. The same thing holds for the liberal and radical.*[42]

But how many teachers understood their own society? How many were not "unfortunately somewhat given to wanting to be told what to do . . . ?" Far too many were poorly prepared; they bristled with methodological acumen but lacked clear sense of the purposes of method. "What will it profit a man to do this, that, and the other specific thing, if he has no clear idea of why he is doing them, no clear idea of the way they bear upon actual conditions and of the end to be reached?" Teachers must be intellectually competent; they must understand the process of education. They must also have the scholarly tenacity to study their society, its antagonistic forces, its potential future courses. In short, the good teacher is one who in his desire to become enlightened has fashioned a social theory "of which educational theory is a part."[43] If but for one generation, teachers would learn and teach "not merely how society *is* going, but how it *might* be intelligently directed, then," Dewey wistfully added, "I should have no fear about the future of democracy."[44] Adequate teaching depended upon more —and more broadly educated—intelligent teachers who possessed social vision and not a little courage.

Seldom in history had so much been expected of the school teacher. Seldom, when set against these lofty expectations, had teachers looked so inept. In effect, Dewey's preachments amounted to indictments of teacher education in particular and the destructiveness of all academic dualisms, as between the "liberal" and "technical," that flourished in academe.

We have largely ignored the details of Dewey's pedagogical views in favor of this cursory exploration of the Great Community he envisioned. Necessarily ignored too have been the developments of Progressive Education and Life Adjustment Education with which Dewey's name has become so popularly linked.[45] For present limited purposes one should note, however, a peculiar irony in the anxious reappraisals of Progressive Education and Life Adjustment Education since 1957 and Sputnik. Those who persist in a defense of Deweyan educational ideals have regularly ignored or failed to make explicit the relationship Dewey insisted upon establishing between educational and social theories. The strange anomaly of John Dewey in the mid-twentieth century is that only the reactionaries of the political right have regularly identified and publicly described the radical inclinations of Dewey's thought since World War I.[46] In their frenzy, amounting at times to group paranoia, American rightists have failed monumentally to discriminate between actual educational developments in twentieth-century America and Dewey's notions of a suitable education. But it is not to the credit of those who continue to find their own social purposes growing out of Dewey's to note that rightists have made the more serious attempts publicly to analyze Dewey's radical educational and cultural purposes. Where Deweyan ideas still survive in unregenerate Schools of Education, where he has not been supplanted by those who treat educational processes in a vacuum innocent of social purpose, one suspects that his writings have been similarly edited and truncated. Thus Dewey has largely become the soft-hearted benignitarian, the immobilized cultural relativist who preached "learn by doing" and "child-centeredness." Tiresomely erroneous and timidly misleading clichès survive as perhaps the inevitably misleading legacy of one who ceased to be a man and became a symbol in his own lifetime. "And it is difficult now," Columbia University philosopher Charles Frankel mused in 1960, "to remember that John Dewey was a man, not an institution, a philosopher, and not a social movement."[47]

•

CHAPTER FIVE

Babies, Bombs, and Business

•

The great stream of time and earthly things will sweep on just the same in spite of us. It is only in imagination that we stand by and look at and criticize it and plan to change it. Everyone of us is . . . in the stream and is swept along with it.

WILLIAM GRAHAM SUMNER

That the course of destiny may be altered by individuals no wise evolutionist ought to doubt.

WILLIAM JAMES

In 1957 James B. Conant began a series of studies of American education which, in time, led him to consider the American high school curriculum, the quality and relevance of slum and suburban education, the preparation of teachers, the debates about the teaching of reading and about vocational education, and the politics of American education. His decision to conduct these studies, and the tone of his reports, made clear a sense of urgency about the reform of the schools. He was not alone in reflecting this urgency. Such mass periodicals as *Time* and *Life*, federal agencies ranging in purpose from the C.I.A. to the Atomic Energy Commission, the major philanthropic foundations, and dozens of scholars and prominent laymen also revealed a near-desperate concern that our educational institutions were not as productive—in terms of turning out highly skilled and well-disciplined manpower—as they must be made if the United States were to meet the economic, political, and military challenges confronting it.

The particular criticisms of the existing school system and the proposed reforms varied, but underlying most of them was an apparent conviction that American education was too easygoing, too playful, and that in the effort to make schooling pleasant educators had failed to take seriously enough their obligation to develop socially productive skills and attitudes. The critics of the 1950's and 1960's were echoing much of the educational ideology with which we have largely dealt.

It has been mostly the ideology of men concerned with building community in the context of ethnic, regional, religious, social class, and partisan conflicts that has been perceived as threatening the social harmony and even the survival of this nation as a community. It has also often been the ideology of men primarily concerned with the efficiency and productivity of the American people. Among the men whose ideas we have examined, only those like Maclure who wanted to substitute science for the common faith have been concerned with insulating the individual from social pressures for ideological conformity. And even the devotees of science sang the praises of production and efficiency.

We have so far largely ignored the lonely voices of pre-existentialist thinkers: of men like Herman Melville, Henry Thoreau and, to some extent, Ralph Waldo Emerson who saw community pressure and the emphasis on social productivity and efficiency as destructive of the individual's unique sense of self, of his highly personal aspirations, and of his integrity. Such men, we have assumed, were somewhat out of the mainstream of American thought in the first century of the national era.

What is, and is not, in the mainstream is probably a function of the way most men perceive the press of society on them. In some eras, and for some people, social forces are perceived as facilitating the realization of their own aspirations. In other eras (we believe increasingly in our own) growing numbers of men perceive societal pressures for efficiency and order as destructive of their selves. Many factors are no doubt involved in determining how men in a particular era regard such societal forces.

In a paradoxical manner, American public schools between 1930 and 1942 developed a relatively relaxed atmosphere and seemed to encourage students to examine and explore their own interests and their social commitments in a leisurely way. It seems paradoxical that education became playful and leisurely in the face of the brutal economic situation Americans then faced. Our bias tells us that freetime was made available for the wrong reasons, and that the educational programs set up were often trivial so far as encouraging a confrontation with crucial existential problems is concerned.

But leisure was, nonetheless, available, the pressure for social productivity was relaxed, and many schoolmen did turn their attention to helping individuals acquire self-understanding even though it might have been at the expense of competency. We find it interesting to examine the way leisure for education was used in the 1930's and to ask the reasons for the relatively dramatic shift from the relaxed attitudes of the 1930's to the urgency of the 1960's. We believe part of the explanation for the shift lies in simple demographic and technological facts: the pressures for scientific and technical skill to apply the new technology and produce the new weapons on the one hand, and fluctuations in birth rate and longevity on the other.

I

In a letter to his brother, William James once expressed a determination to forge his theory ruthlessly in the face of "brute facts" of life. The concept of "brute facts," as related to social theory, intrigues. To examine the educational atmosphere of the 1930's in contrast with that of the 1960's against a background of brute facts of demography and technology is an interesting game for one concerned with the function of ideological rhetoric in social change.

One such brute fact is that somewhere in the 1940's the ratio of people in the "productive age cohort," which we arbitrarily define as those between nineteen and sixty-five years of age, to those in the "dependent age cohorts," i.e. zero to nineteen and sixty-five plus, shifted dramatically not only in respect to total percentages but also with respect to direction of change. Provocative is the now apparent second reversal of this trend.

Moreover, with endless possible qualifications, only some of which we have examined, educational rhetoric changed in precisely the way one would logically have predicted its change in light of this demographic shift. One could argue—though we would not—that the rhetoric and the ideology it projected were nothing but rationalizations for practical changes dictated by the brute forces.

As humanistically oriented historians, we approach the factually brutal world of the demographers and the economists with the naiveté as well as the awe of a child. Certain peaks catch the gleaming sun, and we plot our topography in their terms. Those who live in the more subtle shadows of this world know that the most significant topological features lie hidden in the dark caverns, and they may well see that what is a shining peak to us is but illusion. We cannot refute them, but we would argue that the educational polemicists of the twentieth century were as naive as we and responded to their own particular view of the universe.

For example, we shall deal with the employment situation as if it were the same for male and female, black and white. We know of course that it was not; yet until forced by their black brothers many Americans did not see beyond color of skin to color-based differentials in social opportunity. Nor are our eyes yet trained to see the full import of regional variations, or of variations linked to type of industry.

Let us establish a base line for looking at the relationships among demography, technology, and educational rhetoric. In 1890 the "productive-age cohort" constituted 48.5 per cent of the total population. By a gentle slope this figure rose to 55.8 per cent in 1930, and during the next decade it rose more precipitously to 58.7 per cent in 1940. The reversed trend in the 1940's was accelerated in the next decade so that by 1960 the productive age cohort was down to 52.84 per cent. If we assume that these age cohort categories were tight one could have said in 1960 that never since 1905 had so few Americans been expected to support so many.[1]

The categories are not of course tight. Those over sixty-five have always contributed to production as have those under nineteen. So far as the latter are concerned the proportion of youths participating in the labor market steadily declined from 1890 until 1960 save for a brief period of more full employment during World War II.[2] The same is true of Americans aged sixty-five and over.[3]

The productivity of the American system, as measured by the per capita share of the Gross National Product, rose fairly gently from 1890 to 1930, fell precipitously during the 1930's, and save for a brief period of postwar readjustment and a brief recession during the Eisenhower administration rose dramatically from 1935 to the present.[4] With the exception of the Great Depression the level of unemployment was, despite brief and rapid fluctuations, relatively constant. Only four times did it fall below 2 per cent and on two of those occasions we were engaged in war. Only once before 1930 did the unemployment rate exceed 10 per cent.[5]

There is at least one other crucial variable, namely the educational prerequisites for successful employment in various kinds of careers. Since 1910 the proportion of unskilled workers in the labor force has steadily declined while the proportion classified as clerical and professional has steadily increased. Among the skilled workers those whose skill is based on a long apprenticeship and is relatively independent of formal schooling have also tended to decline somewhat at the expense of the semiskilled and professional. In the decades of the 1950's and 1960's this trend became more crucial because the new industries with the greatest growth rate were thought to require a greater proportion of highly educated workers than did the older major industries. That the massive development of such industries—electronics, chemicals, aircraft, space exploration, and atomics—was new in World War II, and that in the postwar era they were strongly committed to "Research and Development," made their need to recruit highly educated manpower particularly acute. It is interesting that the very phrase "research and development" used to describe large industrial enterprises was a function of the postwar era.[6]

Our economist colleagues have reminded us that from the standpoint of theoretical economics it is by no means the case that production of massive quantities of particular goods necessarily requires a huge investment in highly educated manpower. To some extent, at least, managerial reforms or investment in machinery and less skilled manpower can be substituted. Moreover, they argue, it is at least theoretically possible to make such substitutions in certain industries and thereby release for employment in others whatever highly educated manpower is available. These arguments are persuasive; they suggest that the American people have made certain self-fulfilling assumptions about how an economic system can be made more productive. These assumptions about "brute facts" became, we would argue, all-important historical facts in their own right. In discussing them we therefore move into the middle ground between fact and educational rhetoric.

Two related assumptions have been widely accepted at least in twentieth-century America: (a) that social mobility for individuals—and in America social mobility has always involved a large measure of increased standard of living—is significantly dependent on the amount of formal education one has received, and (b) that governmental, business, and industrial investment in highly educated manpower pays off. Once these assumptions were widely accepted it became inescapable that more and more people would seek further formal education and that industry and commerce would compete more and more vigorously for educated manpower.

So much, then, for the demographic and technological trends we wish to consider; we turn to educational rhetoric. In doing so we propose to specify a somewhat a-historical set of categories for the purpose of delineating trends. The categories are a-historical to the extent that they were not used as we define them in the actual educational debates of which we hope to make sense. We want to talk about peoples' reasons for proposing certain changes in schooling, but in so doing we will also talk about what students were told, at least by implication, they stood to gain from effort in school. Conceive, then, a continuum reaching from what at one extreme shall be labelled "purely social productivity values," to what at the other is labelled "purely consummatory values." Quite likely no concrete educational proposal has in the mind of its advocate represented an example of these pure extremes, but one can consider the acquisition of an unpleasant but nonetheless highly marketable vocational skill as approaching the first and the private contemplation of a highly abstract painting as approaching the second. When Rousseau in his *Emile* criticized Plato for educating the "citizen" first, that is for educating primarily with respect to one's social function, he had evoked something of what we mean by social productivity values; when he proposed instead that attention be given first to the creation of "the man," that is to the development of self-trust and to the understanding and acceptance of one's own deepest aspirations and commitments, he appealed to what we are calling "consummatory values." Of course both Plato and Rousseau believed that in the long run enlightened self-interest and the efficient performance of one's social functions are complementary, if not identical. Most twentieth-century American educators have argued similarly. Yet particular proposals can, we believe, be classified as tending toward one or the other poles of this continuum. Moreover, if one examines successive decades in this century we think he can find clear overall movement between these poles. The argument is that these are precisely the movements one would have predicted in light of the demographic and economic facts noted.

II

The years from 1900 until World War I were years of steady but moderate growth in per capita production. The productive age cohort was rising moderately and the unemployment rate was significant but not alarming. There was sufficient job pressure that legislation designed to remove adolescents from the labor market seemed reasonable. Given the American faith in education as a means of social mobility it made sense for the young to extend their stay in school. Much of the increased productivity of the era was a function of the continued rationalization of industry; this was the era of the efficiency movement, e.g. time and motion studies and the consulting firm, in the economy.[7] No war tested the

American conscience until late in the period, and the most serious of urban problems seemed resolvable if we could find ways of inducting immigrants from abroad and migrants from the rural areas into the economy of the growing urban centers.

The emphasis in educational rhetoric was on what we call the social productivity side of the continuum. To be sure school practices in most places changed little—they rarely change rapidly—and a few romantically oriented educators followed the lead of Francis W. Parker in speaking of child-centered schools. Yet the voices most clearly heard and heeded in legislative and business circles were those calling for vocational education or for training in a kind of citizenship that did not include criticism of the system. The counseling movement, despite the humanitarian biases of such leaders as Eli Weaver, had not yet assumed the "self-realization" cloak it was later to wear. It was itself part of the efficiency movement, an effort to fit each youngster into his proper slot in the social machinery.

It was true that each youngster in the Gary, Indiana, schools, under William Wirt's allegedly "progressive" system, had some participation in determining the rate at which he moved through the curriculum. Yet that system itself epitomized the efficiency movement in its watchful calculation of input-output. Carefully assessed "input and output" calculations lend themselves to handling productivity values; they become a bit sticky when what we call consummatory values are involved.[8] Significantly, the early John Dewey praised this Gary system.

The John Dewey who at the turn of the century wrote *School and Society* and *The Child and the Curriculum* spoke as if enhanced quality of life, rather than mere increased productivity, were his goal. But it is significant that he viewed the study of the processes of producing and distributing goods and services as the most promising core for a curriculum. As we have seen during the 1920's Dewey became progressively more disillusioned with America's institutional life, and by 1928 was describing it as unconscionably destructive of what we are labelling consummatory values. Only after being disillusioned by World War I, stung by the criticism of his erstwhile disciples Randolph Bourne and Lewis Mumford, and appalled at the consequences of the great depression did he turn to *Art as Experience* (1934), the first book in which he wrestled deeply with the problem of consummatory values. His radical political critique emerged, as we have seen, in the 1920's and 1930's.

There was brief depression attending the reorganization of the economy after World War I. By 1924, however, we had returned to a situation quite like that of the prewar decades. The economy, to be sure, was somewhat more heated up; the standard of living rose more rapidly, and the unemployment rate was lower. Social productivity values still dominated educational rhetoric. The most influential professional educator was Edward L. Thorndike, whose general social values (those described by Merle Curti in his *Social Ideas of American Educators,* that is to say) were consistent with those of America's industrial and political leaders. The efficiency movement now bred a rash of new instruments to measure aptitude in terms of precisely defined behaviors, to design textbooks in terms of word count, and to construct curricula in terms of the traits and skills actually demanded of Americans in filling their prescribed social functions. Perhaps Franklin Bobbitt was the leading curriculum designer, but such men as David Snedden, who shared many views with Thorndike and Bobbitt, had the ear of the powerful.[9]

There was one relatively new consummatory theme in the background of debate in the 1920's. A precious circle of avant garde artists and intellectuals in the urban areas began to cry for "creative expression" and for liberation from taboos which they saw entrenched in the American Puritan tradition. Among them were Margaret Naumberg, who established a psychoanalytically oriented school in New York, and her husband Waldo Frank, who edited the *Seven Arts.* Certainly the avant garde stress on "self-realization" and "creative expression" as educational objectives reflected a degree of nausea with the dominant culture as they perceived it. In the case of Randolph Bourne, one of their early, and prematurely deceased, heroes, disillusionment with American participation in the war was the final straw.[10] Ironically greater knowledge of European events, which the war produced, may also have heightened awareness of America's cultural narrowness. It had never been hidden from sensitive intellectuals.

Insofar as the economic factors under consideration affected the values of this avant garde group—and we grant that the affect may have been minimal—our guess is that their response adumbrated one we will see in the case of bourgeois youngsters in the 1960's. There was sufficient affluence in the middle 1920's that job insecurity no longer spurred bright and moderately well-educated youngsters. Moreover a middle class rapidly becoming more affluent, and itself believing prosperity was here to stay, did consume its wealth in an obscenely philistine manner. That this particular group of select young people had been exposed to the social reform agitation of early decades and may well have at least learned to see the suffering of the poor could have made the life styles of their elders especially obnoxious. Maybe a society affluent as was middle class urban America in 1926, and unprepared as it was to use this affluence well, simply creates a boring pattern of life. Possibly what we now call "alienation" has a large component of simple boredom combined with leisure. In any case the call for creative expression affected few American educators in the 1920's. The world of expectations and aspirations turned in 1930. The poor starved, the merely affluent became poor, only the very rich got richer. The average per capita share of the national product fell from $850 to less than $600, and the unemployment figure rose to almost 25 per cent. At a time when jobs were scarce the ratio of those in the productive age cohort was approaching the highest to be reached in American history up to the present. Young people were certainly not wanted in the labor pool and a series of New Deal legislative acts, e.g. social security and the C.C.C., were designed for, among other purposes, the removal of the old and the young from the labor market. Since unemployment affected the professionally and highly skilled vocations as well as the unskilled ones, there existed essentially no vocationally oriented school program that would guarantee access to employment. Even in an increasing number of homes unemployed adolescents and young adults saw themselves as an economic burden to their once reasonably well-to-do parents.

For the educators the old goads has lost their sting: One could no longer promise economic success or even appeal to a sense of duty to produce for society. At the same time it seemed important to keep youngsters off the streets, where bad habits might be learned, as well as out of the labor market. We suspect many youngsters, with their less well developed sense of historical time, had even less confidence that the future would be better than did their now disillusioned parents. Their's was an unwanted generation, where possible held in school—to their desperation and out of the desperation of their elders.

Under these conditions there occurred, understandably enough, a significant shift to consummatory values. Guidance counselors began to talk less of vocational choice and more of "self-realization." Into the social studies courses crept units on how to get along with parents and peers; while the literature anthologies, though keeping many of the standard items, arranged them into units focused on problems of adolescents. Most notably, perhaps, extra-curricular activities moved to the center of the stage. If preparation for a band festival, a pep-rally to arouse enthusiasm for the athletic team, or a school play practice sometimes got in the way of a vocational agriculture or advanced mathematics class, a good case could be made for sacrificing the class. At no other time in our history, we suspect, had it seemed so important that students enjoy what they were about. Given the economic situation how else save by prison methods could they be kept in school?

Three books serve as illustrative of the new depression-borne rhetoric concerning education. Two of these were published under the auspices of the American Youth Commission of the American Council on Education: one by Harl Douglass, *Secondary Education for Youth in Modern America* (1937), and the other by Homer P. Rainey with collaborators, *How Fare American Youth* (1938). The third, written for the Educational Policies Commission largely by William G. Carr, was *The Purposes of Education in American Democracy* (1928). In contrast with the rhetoric of the 1960's these books are all remarkable because of the stress placed on such objectives as "self-realization," "human relations," "health," and the "effective use of leisure time." Such objectives had of course been stressed earlier in, for example, the reports of the N.E.A.'s Commission on the Reorganization of the Secondary School Curriculum in 1918. But what had been an eddy then was in the late 1930's the main current of educational rhetoric.

With some educators and more students, especially at the college level, a strident call for social reform was heard in the 1930's. We stretch the category of consummatory values to include this since we have already defined the old style preparation for citizenship as a productive value. Yet the new citizenship education demanded by such people as Harold Rugg and John Dewey was different in that the emphasis was less on how to succeed in the system than on how to make the system more responsive to human aspirations. They were not asking how to make the system more productive; they were asking how to make it more humane in their terms.

We depart from strict chronology to discuss a strangely paradoxical relationship between radical student activism of the 1920's and 1930's and that of the 1950's and 1960's. The radicals of the 1920's faced an affluent society. For middle-class children the problem of economic security and vocation was a modest one to say the least. Particularly those attending the more expensive private colleges and universities confronted a problem not of survival but of boredom, triviality, and conflict between the putative spiritual values and the philistine consummatory behavior of their parents. Moderately or very wealthy students who did not embrace the life style of the newly wealthy turned to bohemianism: to art, psychoanalysis, and the "creative life." Such students, however, constituted a very small group compared with those who accepted the dominant work ethic or made their peace with conspicuous consumption.

In the 1960's students from wealthy middle-class families also rebelled in somewhat bohemian directions. However, there has been, it seems to us, a quality of anxiety and despair in the "flower-

children" that was less marked in the case of their bohemian predecessors, though the economic situation faced by the two groups was
likely perceived in similar terms. If our hunch concerning the difference in anxiety level is correct, we are inclined to explain it in
terms of pervasive anxiety related to the great depression, the Nazi
movement, atomic warfare, and continued international tensions.
The revolutionary shift in the aspirations of the blacks is an important part of the new picture as is the development of television
as a medium more poignantly revealing the presence of conflict.

We see the "flower-children" and their more ideologically
oriented age-mates in the existentialist left as the product of an
economic situation something like that of the 1920's, and we see
their behavior as somewhat analogous to that of the "bohemians."
But the radical student movement of the 1960's also has a component made up of disillusioned blacks and their sympathizers. Interestingly enough the blacks of the 1960's perceive themselves in a
situation not unlike that faced by student radicals in the 1930's, although it may be harder for them to accept because it is more
clearly disciminatory.

What student radicals faced in the 1930's was the death of
opportunity. Despite the American rhetoric about the efficacy of
hard work, frugality, and education as insurers of economic mobility, two generations of college students faced a situation in which
this rhetoric was patently false. They turned to revolt against the
system, not to productive careers within it. Fortunately, for those
who consider the system essentially desirable, prosperity, full employment, and a sense of shared national purpose returned with
the War and most of the revolutionary careers were aborted.

When in the 1930's simple economic depression had closed off
opportunity to a major portion of youth, lower and middle class,
black and white, alike, simple economic reform seemed a sensible
response. When in the 1960's affluence created a sense of potential
opportunity and abundance for all, it was clear that something in
addition to simple economic reform was indicated. The black radicals and their allies in the 1960's focus their attention on a situation
that appears in some ways analogous to that faced by student radicals in the 1930's. Like their 1930 predecessors they agitate for
political and economic reform. But just as we see the radicalism of
the "flower-children" as somewhat more anxious and complex than
that of the "bohemians," so is the radicalism of the blacks and their
allies more anxious and complex than that of the 1930 "Marxists."

We return to the chronological path from which we digressed
to discuss student radicalism in the 1920's, 1930's, and 1960's.
While America abandoned herself to war and reconstruction in
the 1940's, the economic and demographic world turned again,

almost unnoticed. For the first time in this century, if not in American history, growth in the dependent age cohorts outran that in the productive age cohorts. The baby boom and the geriatric revolution were upon us. Between 1940 and 1960 the relative size of the productive age cohort dropped by 6 per cent. In these two decades the change was almost equal in magnitude to that experienced in reverse direction in the previous four decades.

The most immediate impact of this change on education was of course felt in the shortage of school building space, a shortage made more acute because first depression, then—and much more markedly—war, had prevented cities from keeping pace. Lack of space, and accelerating building costs, were in themselves enough to make people ask if all that had conventionally been done in schools was really necessary.

The teacher shortage was the next apparent consequence of the new situation. Again there had been a lack of replacement during the war years, but more important the new affluence and veterans educational benefits, which gave many men a chance to prepare for more lucrative vocations, drained off large numbers of potential replacements. As we shall see the educators continued for a time to think in terms of the prewar situation; but more critically for the teacher supply situation public authorities were incredibly slow to realize that a new salary structure had emerged in American life. The same businessman who in employing management personnel quickly responded to a highly competitive labor market failed as a member of a school board or state legislature to see that potential teachers had the same favorable labor market.

During the war the per capita share of the Gross National Product had grown from $800 to $1300, and after a brief period of readjustment it climbed again to in excess of $1400 by 1957. These, by the way, are reported in terms of 1929 dollars and the increase is not therefore a function of devalued currency.

Unemployment even in the recession years of 1955 and 1962 never rose higher than about 7 per cent. By 1950 the major industrial and professional groups all began to feel the manpower pinch, particularly with respect to highly educated persons. By 1950 President Eisenhower, of Columbia University, had launched a major manpower study under the direction of Eli Ginsberg, and the C.I.A. had issued its first ominous report about the Soviet threat to overtake the United States in its supply of such human resources. The National Science Foundation had also begun to express grave concern about the growing shortage of scientific and engineering personnel.[11]

Note that these events antedate the launching of sputnik by a half decade. If a Soviet scientific and technological feat had any catalytic influence on the reappraisal of American education it was not Sputnik; rather, it was the making of an atomic bomb years before our experts considered the Soviets capable of such a feat. If we were to name the three men who had the major influence in convincing the leaders of American society that something was seriously wrong with our educational system they would be James B. Conant, Admiral Hyman Rickover, and Professor Jerrold Zacharias, of the Massachusetts Institute of Technology. All had been active in the federal scientific-engineering establishment during and after World War II, and all were in some way involved in atomic energy use. It is reasonable to hypothesize that the comparative scientific-technological strengths of the United States and the Soviet Union were a matter of grave concern to them; it is not surprising that they couched their pleas for educational reforms in terms of national defense and national duty.

Yet we think it a mistake to assume that the call for reform, even on the part of these men, was a simple response to the Russian bomb, or to Sputnik, or to the threat of eventual war with the Soviets. The Cold War was of great importance, but part of its importance may have derived from its relationship to American yearning for the "white cliffs of Dover" and to the frustration of that yearning.

The years of World War II were years of enforced saving and deferred consumption for most Americans. Sufficient demand for refrigerators, automobile, and a host of other goods was built up by itself to have heated up the economy once peace returned. Perhaps just as importantly scientific capital had been invested in war technology, and a number of vast new consumer industries—especially the electronics industry, from which computers and television sets were shortly to flow—waited but for peace to flourish.

In the early, hard, and discouraging years of the war Americans like Britons sang of hope for the bluebirds' return to Dover; in the later years of the war Americans drooled over pictures of the home and automobile of the future. Assuming, or at least hoping for, continued cooperation and peace with their only apparent powerful potential enemy, the Soviet Union, it seemed nothing was likely to bar the way to infinite progress and prosperity. It is in the context of disillusionment and frustrated hope that Cold War anger and anxiety must be viewed.

Abundance in fact returned, but not security. "The Age of Innocence" out of which a few Americans had moved in earlier decades was now past for many. In the late 1950's and the 1960's Americans spent and played as frantically as in the 1920's, but now with repeated and frightened glances over their shoulders. Responsible men, self-selected and publicly affirmed as defenders of the republic, its virtue, and its prosperity, had little time for triviality or play. The intellectual and moral resources of the gifted young, they believed, must be cultivated as quickly and efficiently as possible. A whole new subfield of economics, the economics of human resource development, was born. "It is time," announced *Life* magazine, "to close the circus that is American education." More scientists, doctors, engineers, lawyers, technicians, teachers, nurses, maybe even poets were needed to fill the shrinking ranks of the productive cohort.

Not all the cries for educational reform came from people close to the political-industrial-military complex. During what we have called the productivity-oriented era of pre-World War I, such humanists as Irving Babbitt and Paul Elmer More had castigated the educational reformers for their lack of consummatory, e.g. aesthetic, values and for their crass commercialism. When in the 1930's education turned somewhat toward consummatory values, these proved to successors of More, e.g., Robert Hutchins and Norman Foerster, to be the wrong consumer values; they were values which these critics saw as lacking in aesthetic sensitivity and intellectual rigor. When World War II ended, Albert Lynd, Mortimer Smith, and Arthur Bestor were early in the field of criticism of what they saw as triviality or aimlessness in American education. Though not agreeing with each other on many points, these three generations of critics shared a generally humanist point of view and criticized American education as having false aims (or no aims at all) and as having students engage too much in trivia.[12] They did not, however, place major value on the development of marketable vocational skills.

III

Those people we see as "humanists," e.g. Bestor, and those we see involved in a new efficiency movement, e.g. Rickover, in the 1960's joined in applauding the polemic literature distributed by the Council for Basic Education.[13] All wanted to "close the circus." Yet we repeat the opinion that with men of power in this society those educational critics who wanted to produce highly skilled manpower in the interest of national defense and the national economy have had the greatest influence. We included in this category, Rickover, Conant, and Zacharias; yet when one looks at their proposals the dangers, even the injustices, of putting thoughtful men in categories become clear.

The case of James B. Conant illustrates the change in values between the 1930's and the 1960's as well as the dangers of categorization. His scholarly field, physical chemistry, was one that developed at the outset in close relationship to industry, and though his early distinguished work on photosynthesis was certainly "pure research," he turned as well to applied chemistry. In World War I he served in the army's chemical warfare division and after the war established a firm producing explosives. That venture ended in disaster when an explosion wrecked the plant, killing his partner. The financial loss was partly recouped by the sale of patent rights for certain chemical processes of industrial value that he had developed. In connection with World War II he served with Bernard Baruch in the rubber survey that explored the possibilities of synthetic replacements for the natural rubber denied the United States by Japanese advances in Southeast Asia. His work in coordinating the Nation's scientific efforts in the war, including the development of the atomic bomb, is widely known. When the war ended he was a central figure in continued deliberations concerning the role of the federal government in the advancement of science, and the role of science in the advancement of the national interest. Before, during, and after the war he was among those most deeply concerned with the effective utilization of human resources, and in this connection was involved in decisions concerning the draft and military training.

Before the American entry into World War II, Conant had been a leader of groups dedicated to encouraging the United States to assist the allies against Germany, and as the war drew to a close he became United States High Commissioner to Germany and then first United States Ambassador to West Germany. In these positions, as well as in his role in the development of the Atomic Energy Commission, he observed at first hand the growing conflicts of interests out of which the Cold War emerged.

From the beginning of his career to the present, then, Conant has interacted with those people most directly concerned with production, national defense, and citizenship. He has also been an extraordinarily energetic man, with strong intellectual interests and a keen sense of duty. One would expect such a man to have low tolerance for what appeared to be time-wasting, consummatory-oriented educational practices. Conant has never been the kind of romantic to whom it is enough that people, including students, enjoy themselves and keep out of trouble. To him, as to his Puritan forebearers, "life is earnest."[14]

Yet his values were never merely productivity ones. A strong sense of community, an awareness of and appreciation for differences among people, and a sense of social justice emerged early. Well before he became President of Harvard University in 1935 he had begun quoting Jefferson's arguments for equality of opportunity as well as for cultivation of the natural aristocracy. Moreover, perhaps as a reflection of his empirical bent, he soon developed a sense of social realities.

After becoming President of Harvard he engaged in three efforts relative to our concern. Believing that Harvard College should not remain essentially a finishing school for the sons of the New England aristocracy, he launched a program of national scholarships to bring talented though not wealthy students from across the nation to Cambridge. Quite likely a desire both to extend opportunity and to broaden the American sense of community were involved in this decision. Believing that general education should have closer connections with the lives and aspirations of students he began to mobilize faculty thought in behalf of a new general education program. Believing that Harvard University had an obligation with respect to American public education he turned to the reform of the Harvard Graduate School of Education and began to participate in activities of the professional educators.

From 1942 to 1963 he served with interruptions as a member of the Educational Policy Commission, a national body of distinguished citizens sponsored jointly by the National Education Association and the American Association of School Administrators. If one wants to follow the major concerns of leaders of public education, tempered somewhat by the convictions of powerful laymen interested in public education, volumes issued by the Educational Policies Commission constitute one of the prime sources. Of these volumes the most interesting in the context of this essay is *Education for All American Youth*, initiated in 1942 and published in 1944 during Conant's membership on the commission.

In the 1960's, *Education for All American Youth* has a curiously anachronistic quality. For one thing its authors did not anticipate the population changes that in fact occurred. Moreover, they chose for artistic reasons to open the volume with an imagined "future historian's account of the postwar years," which they hoped would not be written, and a second account, which they hoped would. Neither closely conforms to what actually occurred.

More importantly the flavor of the volume, despite extended statements about the importance of intellectual development and vocational preparation, is that of the 1930's. There is the same "democracy" of values among educational objectives and subjects. This is to say that the same weight appears to be given such topics as "understanding the significance of the family," or using leisure time well, as to understanding the methods of science and the social sciences. Exemplary units for the tenth grade "common learnings core" include "the American city at play," "housing in relation to family life," and "community health conditions and needs." And, of course, what is recommended after the completion of the initially preplanned unit is to be decided by "your class and your teacher," i.e. "pupil-teacher planning."

The authors were quick to point out that serious intellectual effort, drawing on advanced scholarship, would be expected in the study of such units. In so doing they reflected a by then old conviction that the "subject-centered" curriculum was not an effective way to induct the young into the life of the mind. The point is not whether they were right or wrong; it is that this way of talking about educating characterized the 1930's but is rarely heard save with disdain from such people as Rickover and Zacharias, or even from Conant in the 1960's.

Conant could not have participated at any great length in deliberations concerning the *Education for All American Youth;* he was much too busy with the bomb. But he did strongly endorse the E.P.C. volume in his Sachs Lecture at Teachers College, Columbia University in 1946.[15] Moreover, the basic idea of organizing instruction in terms of "the problems of living," should not have been obnoxious to him. In the 1920's with his old secondary school science teacher Newton Henry Black he had written a very popular high school chemistry textbook the very title of which, *Practical Chemistry, Fundamental Facts and Applications to Modern Life,* reflected a predisposition toward "problem-centered" instruction. Finally, in the Sachs lecture he also strongly endorsed the then recently published *Harvard Report on General Education,* which he described as in the same spirit as *Education for All American Youth.* The difference, he argued, reflected only the differences in the types of students and life aspirations with respect to which the two volumes were written. A conviction that education must account for such differences in aptitudes and aspirations runs through his writings.

Now the issue involving "child-centered," "subject-centered," and "problem-centered" curricula are not merely matters of educational values. Certainly different positions on these issues do not necessarily correlate with positions on our theoretical social productivity-consummatory continuum of values and rewards. But in the 1950's and 1960's they came to be perceived by many in these terms. "Problem-centered" and "child-centered" curricula were grouped by such critics as Arthur Bestor and Hyman Rickover as examples of "life adjustment education." Many of the earlier social efficiency concerns had been incorporated into the life-adjustment education movement, particularly a concern for vocational efficiency and for civic participation. In the 1950's and 1960's, however, the kinds of vocations in which manpower shortages were most keenly felt were precisely those requiring mastery of mathematics and the sciences. Given the technology of the 1920's "subject-centered" instruction had been viewed by some educators as nonadjustive to the vocational needs of many students; business arithmetic had replaced algebra. In the technological world of the 1960's the older patterns of vocational preparation seemed trivial; the new social efficiency advocates found calculus and physics most important.

The phrase, "life adjustment education," generated in the 1940's but reflecting a 1930's bias, grew out of the problem of what to do about youngsters who were neither retarded nor academically talented or motivated enough to seek out collegiate or rigorous technical training. In the 1930's many students fit this category so far as motivation was concerned, but in the late 1940's it was thought to include the "middle 60 per cent." To many critics of the 1950 period, *Education for All American Youth* epitomized the values symbolized by the old life-adjustment education. That Conant endorsed a volume these other critics scorned is evidence that he reflected some of the values prominent in the thought of educators in the 1930's. Indeed, Conant's understanding of the problems the public educators had faced, and his determination to work constructively with them, led to their perception of him as the single friendly powerful critic. Throughout the 1950's public school educators, ever more sorely pressed by opponents, were repeatedly to express thanks to deity for Conant.

Yet, as we have pointed out, Conant had always been concerned with the cultivation of an intellectual aristocracy, had always viewed the educational enterprise as a serious one to be tested largely in terms of efficiency. Though his subsequent writings were continually to emphasize the community building function of the schools, he did begin to stress more consistently the acquisition of highly trained intellectual skills for the gifted and the acquisiton of vocational skills for all. From his books one must infer that for the gifted this involved a "subject-centered" curriculum. That is to say students should study science, as such, the social science, as such, and the humanities, as such.

He also became increasingly restless about instruction or guidance that seemed to serve entertainment or "self-realization" values not clearly related to greater social efficiency. The marching bands and the music festivals in the 1930's had been perceived by many as valuable social experiences, enhancing the child's sense of belongingness and participation, to use the kinds of terms then popular. At least by the late 1950's Conant came to view them as trivial and wasteful of time; perhaps he had always considered them such. It was not that he opposed the serious study of music by talented youngsters; quite the contrary. He merely thought the marching bands gave bad performances of marginal music, at best, and that their training consumed an inordinate amount of time.

Perhaps more than that of any single man Conant's influence was crucial in the decision to invest massive federal funds in the training of guidance workers. Yet it is clear from his various descriptions of the guidance function that he had in mind something of the kind of educational and vocational advisement that had characterized the guidance movement in the 1920's. Counseling closely related to psychological therapy, whether Rogerian or neo-Freudian, had fit the mood and the conditions of the 1930's, and in the guidance profession, which now chose to call itself the "counseling" profession, this trend was augmented throughout the 1950's and into the 1960's. But the new counselors were not investing their time as Conant had obviously hoped they would. If we are correct in arguing that the basic trend of the 1950-1960 decades was toward social efficiency values, one has to explain why the counseling people continued to move in a counter direction. Our hunch, which we will develop subsequently, is that students in the 1950's and 1960's developed more acute intrapersonal conflicts requiring some form of near-therapy. And we suspect that the very emphasis on productivity values in the rest of their school program played a part in this phenomenon.

We are not certain that Conant's values changed significantly between 1930 and 1965; but it is quite clear that he perceived the two situations very differently, requiring different educational emphases.[16] The tone of publications of the Educational Policies Commission, at a time when he was most active, began to shift fairly abruptly after the publication of *Education for All American Youth*. In 1951, for example, under Conant's chairmanship the Commission joined with the American Council of Education to publish *Education and National Security*. Though citizenship and human relations values were still espoused, the increased concern with manpower, particularly highly educated or well-trained manpower, is in dramatic contrast to that found in earlier volumes. Later volumes such as *The Contemporary Challenge to American Education* (1958) emphasize guidance and the education of the gifted in the context of the growing threat of conflict with the Soviet Union. Conant's own recent books *The American High School Today* (1958), *The Child, The Parent, and the State* (1959), and *Slums and Suburbs* (1961) reflect the same growing urgency about the national interest in intellectual resources. Particularly notable in this respect is the strong emphasis, in *The American High School Today*, on the obligation of the gifted to carry heavy loads in "solid subjects" that prepare for socially productive careers.

Conant was not a member of the Educational Policies Commission when it issued *Manpower and Education* in 1956. This volume, which presents the same kinds of statistical data we have used, is a prime example of the new attitude toward productivity and consummatory values. If *The Purposes of Education in American Democracy* reflects the atmosphere of the 1930's, and *Education for All American Youth* that of the transitional 1940's, *Manpower and Education* mirrors the 1960's.

In a number of crucial matters the rhetoric of Admiral Hyman Rickover differs from that of Conant, and there is also in Rickover's case some ambiguity to be explained when one tries to classify him as representing a new social efficiency trend. In the almost archaic language of nineteenth-century exponents of liberal education, Rickover defends the study of Greek and Latin classics. His is a kind of language which Conant vigorously eschews as lacking in precise referents. Moreover, Rickover is quite willing to sacrifice the comprehensive high school, which Conant sees as valuable in terms of building a sense of community, and therefore of belongingness, among the various segments of American society. At least as far as the school is concerned, Rickover views the development of intellectual talent as the sole legitimate end.[17]

Rickover entered the educational reform movement out of frustration during his recruiting technological and scientific talent for the production of the atomic submarine, and his major books on education are based overwhelmingly on the argument that in competition with the Soviet Union all our available brainpower must be developed and devoted to the national interest. At times, as in *Education and Freedom,* even the case for the classics is made in terms of the production of more effective engineers. His power in the educational reform movement has been based not only on prestige derived from the development of the *Nautilus,* but as well on his avid testimony before admiring congressmen.

To place Jerrold Zacharias in the new social efficiency category demands what may be unwarranted inference. Unlike Conant and Rickover he has made few published statements about educational values. He is a professor at the Massachusetts Institute of Technology and has had very strong support from the federal scientific establishment, particularly the National Science Foundation. He has been a member of the President's Science Advisory Committee and has chaired a Panel on Educational Research and Development, which in 1964 advised the U.S. Commissioner of Education, the National Science Foundation, and the Special Assistant to the President for Science and Technology.[18] Moreover, the "new curriculum movement," of which he has been by all odds the most vigorous agent, has throughout been "discipline-oriented," in contrast to the "child-centered" or "problem-centered" orientation of the 1930's and 1940's.

The theoretical rhetoric of the new curriculum movement has

come from Jerome Bruner of Harvard, who has on occasion worked with Zacharias. It was he who popularized the ideas of the "structure of the disciplines" and the "discovery method," which characterize talk about the new movement. Yet we cannot comfortably place Bruner in the new social efficiency camp; there is too much almost Freudian "self-understanding" in his arguments, and there is a sensitivity to artistic and poetic impulses which we see as falling on the consummatory end of our continuum. If Bruner does not represent a movement back to social efficiency values, it is hazardous to assert that Zacharias does. Nonetheless, we do assert that regardless of Zacharias' intentions, the support for the new curriculum movement has come largely out of a concern with the national interest in the use of scientifically and technologically trained talent.

We should describe the "new curriculum movement" since we assert that it was a characteristic response to conditions in the 1950's and 1960's, and also since the making of "new curricula" had been almost a fetish among professional educators in the preceding decades. What sets the "new curriculum" apart from its predecessors is partly its "discipline," i.e. conventional "subject matter," orientation. But it is also characterized by a marked involvement of university scholars in the selection from their own disciplines of concepts and materials to be included. Conversely, the professors of education who led earlier curricular revision movements have played a relatively small role in the new movement.

Zacharias was not the first scholar from a university academic discipline to launch a new postwar curriculum movement. Prior to his involvement, a group at the University of Illinois in 1951 established a Committee of School Mathematics (UICSM). Zacharias entered the picture in 1956 with an attempt to build a new physical sciences curriculum. His early attempts to combine chemistry and physics were unsuccessful and his first completed project was a physics course (PSSC) developed in 1957. Since that time the chemists have developed two new curricula while the biological scientists have developed three separate programs ostensibly oriented around certain common assumptions and concepts. There are now a number of competing curricula in mathematics, the social sciences, and foreign languages.[19]

Besides his function as a promoter of these new programs, Zacharias has also proved highly effective in establishing machinery for the production of new curricula and instructional materials. Educational Services Incorporated, which he established after experience with PSSC, became the model. Distinguished scholars, classroom teachers, experts in the production of audio and visual materials, and research people were here mobilized in a continuous operation of developing new courses of study and guides for teaching them. In addition to continued work on science instruction, the Zacharias group moved extensively into mathematics and the social sciences. Educational Services Incorporated became the model for the new curriculum centers, and the National Science Foundation became the prime source of support until United States Office of Education research funds became more abundant; Jerrold Zacharias was a powerful figure in both.

One other type of agency with growing influence on education during the 1950's and 1960's should be noticed. It is the new research-and-development-oriented segment of industry. In the 1950's the television industry began to exploit a potential education market; in the same decade and increasingly in the subsequent decade the computer industry moved in to support experimentation in the use of electronic machinery for teaching and school administration. By 1969 several major industries, e.g. Xerox, Raytheon, C.B.S., and General Electric, had gained control of publishing houses and had established education divisions. When Francis Keppel resigned as Commissioner of Education he joined one such corporation; when Louis Bright came to the position of research director for the U.S. Office of Education he came from Westinghouse; when under "Great Society" legislation the job corps was established, a number of private industries took responsibility for establishing camps. The active participation of industrial management in developing curricula, instructional technology, and instructional materials does not of course insure that productivity values will dominate. That such will be the tendency we are, nonetheless, willing to wager.

Whether they used the new curriculum or the old, the schools of the 1960's were clearly more efficient than those of the 1930's had been. Students did more homework, handled more sophisticated concepts, and, if the almost universal testimony of experienced college professors is to be trusted, came to college much better prepared academically than had earlier generations.

By 1960 college authorities were much more concerned with academic aptitude than they had been previously. In the 1930's the major concern of private colleges had been to get enough students to forestall bankruptcy; even such wealthy colleges as Harvard had found themselves in desperate need of more tuition money. By 1960 when potential students far exceeded good college facilities, and potential professors were at ebb tide, the problems were reversed.

Moreover, the financial support for professors had shifted markedly from tuition funds to research funds provided by government and industry. A growing supply of capable research assistants was essential for the major universities if they wanted to keep up this pattern of support. Talented undergraduates, rigorously trained, were the only source of these assistants. To the university professor's delight in having bright students was added a sense of urgency about professional training. As colleges therefore tightened their selection processes, the pressures on the lower schools for efficiency increased.

IV

The reformers of the Post-War II era have had significant impact; a greater share of the nation's intellectual resources is now being cultivated for potential service to national economic and defense needs. But there are side effects of this progress. Three of them particularly interest us: (1) as efficiency criteria are more rigorously applied in opening social mobility through education, the plight of the ghetto black becomes more and not less acute; (2) there is some reason to suspect that an increasing number of bright and articulate young people, perceiving themselves as having been exploited in the social interest, may be choosing to drop out of active employment in the system; and (3) with the reversal of the trend toward expanding the dependency age cohorts at the expense of the productive age cohorts we might soon find ourselves in an age where consummatory values are reasserted in education.

With respect to the status of the ghetto blacks, as the suburban and smaller city schools underwent reforms aimed at creating more efficient producers, the ghetto schools became even more markedly custodial institutions. Their students did not reach the levels of academic achievement on which success in a meritocracy of highly educated people depends. Put bluntly, too few ghetto black children were prepared to meet collegiate standards for admission and retention. Not only had their white competitors enjoyed the advantages inherent in anti-Negro bias; also white schools had been staffed with more highly qualified and stable faculties, thus the students had more highly marketable intellectual skills to sell.

As Conant recommended in *Slums and Suburbs* the ghetto blacks can be given the vocational training needed to secure employment, and this would place them in a significantly better position than that in which they now find themselves. But to expand efforts to provide this kind of education for ghetto blacks while suburban whites are offered excellent training in those intellectual disciplines on which success in prestigious jobs apparently now depends is also to perpetuate a caste society.

For this reason leaders of the black community in the 1960's have demanded both educational reform that will give their children an equal shot at the skilled vocations and a moratorium on rigorously applied academic merit ratings for immediate employment in prestigious posts. As we write, university administrators deliberate about demands to waive the usual admissions requirements and to provide remedial aids to ghetto blacks admitted under the liberalized requirements. Departments on many campuses vigorously seek black professors who meet the normal criteria for employment in major university faculties. The same process is underway in all segments of government and the economy. No one argues that, at least in the short run, the nation's business will be more efficiently conducted by filling critical social roles with academically less well-prepared persons. It is asserted that in the long run continued educational deprivation of the ghetto blacks is expensive as far as national resources are concerned. Yet the basic arguments have to do with the black man's image of himself. Matters of self-image involve what we have classified as consummatory values.

The national need for technologically trained manpower and management personnel has been, we have suggested, behind much of the pressure for educational reform in the past two decades. Probably these needs have been more adequately met than would have been the case without the reforms. At the end of the seventh decade, however, engineering schools are facing an increasing problem of recruiting students, and industrial leaders are complaining that too many bright and well-educated young people are rejecting careers in business and industry. The articulate radical students are providing an explanation, whether real or not.

The radical student rhetoric throughout the sixties has played the theme that American education has sold out to the military-industrial complex; that the students have been exploited in terms of the "national interest," which they perceived as a cover for business and industry. They argue that their personal interests have been ignored, their own voices unheard. Though they might grant that the things they have studied are useful from a productive standpoint, they assert that the same things are irrelevant to their "real" concerns and interests. Though the national leaders in the counseling movement have continued to stress their function in helping students "discover themselves," the student radicals perceive even the counseling centers as engaged in a near conspiracy to sell them out to "the establishment," i.e. to find a calling consistent with "national purpose."

There has developed a coterie of adult educational critics who attempt to express the spirit of student protest. Widely known

members of this coterie are Paul Goodman and Edgar Frieden-
berg, both of whom see the pressure and rigidity of the current
system as destructive of a student's sense of identity. An earlier
critic who evidently did not excite the student radicals (in many
respects his values are conservative) was John Hersey, whose *The
Child Buyer* was a delightful satire on education and the national
purpose.

Men like James B. Conant would be shocked at the charge
that they have exploited and used a generation of students for
social ends which those students would not have chosen. Of the
critics we have specifically cited Conant particularly has opposed a
coercive pedagogy, opting always for a considerable degree of
student choice in subject matter and for persuasion rather than
compulsion with respect to those subjects he thought all students
should have. The pedagogical assumption underlying the works
of Zacharias, i.e. that learning is largely the product of exploratory
behavior and "discovery," seems dependent on the student's freely
abandoning himself to the enterprise. And even Rickover talks of
zest for learning. Yet we believe the rhetoric of the student radicals is in some degree a response to the rhetoric of the reformers
and to the educational environment they helped to create. Preaching about duty and obligation persuades some; it repulses others.

We have argued that the great sense of urgency about the
cultivation of intellectual resources in the last two decades has been
to a degree a function of the demographic-technological situation
—a situation in which a shortage of people in the productive age
cohort coincided with a booming economy and the threat of international war. The demographic trend now seems to be reversing
and it is conceivable that lacking another war the demand for
highly educated manpower may soon slacken. One who regards
this trend with the resignation of William Sumner might well agree
that "The great stream of time and earthly things will sweep on just
the same in spite of us." But those who act upon the belief that
human aspirations are more than mere flotsam in the great stream
will echo William James' terse rejoinder: "That the course of destiny may be altered by individuals no wise evolutionist ought to
doubt."

Demography is not the only critical variable or brute fact. If
it were, and were our thesis of a correlation between demographic
trends and educational rhetoric correct, we should predict as well
as prefer a new age in which consummatory values are reasserted.

CHART I.

RATIO OF PERSONS IN THE PRODUCTIVE AGE COHORT TO THOSE IN
THE DEPENDENCY AGE GROUPS

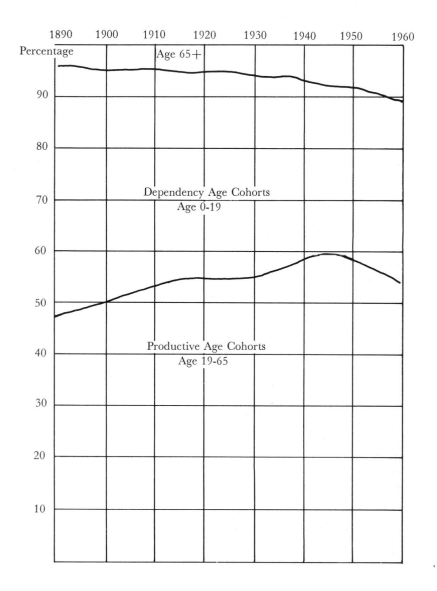

Source: U. S. Census Bureau.

Chart II 139

CHART II.   PERCENTAGE OF YOUTH IN THE LABOR FORCE (AGES 14-19)

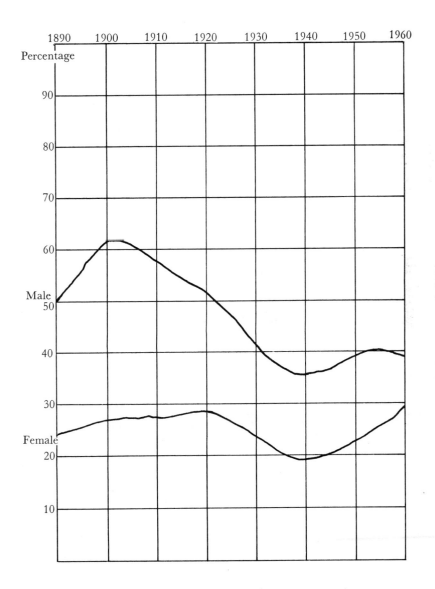

Source: U. S. Census Bureau, *Historical Statistics of the United States*, p. 71 (figures for 1890-1950); and 1960 Census Reports PC2-6A.

CHART III.   PER CAPITA SHARE OF GROSS NATIONAL PRODUCT (1929 DOLLARS)

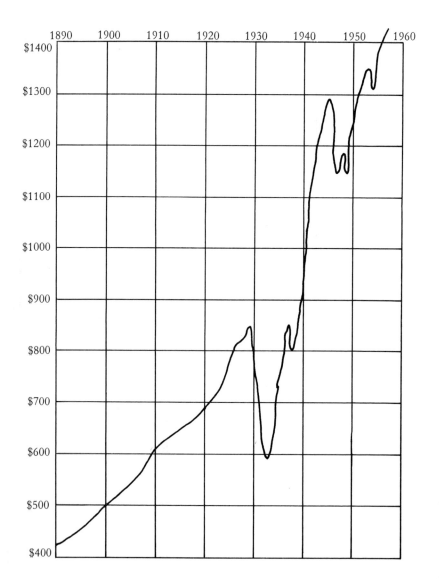

Source: U. S. Census Bureau, *Historical Statistics of the United States*, 1960, p. k39.

Chart IV 141

CHART IV. RATE OF UNEMPLOYMENT, 1900-1967

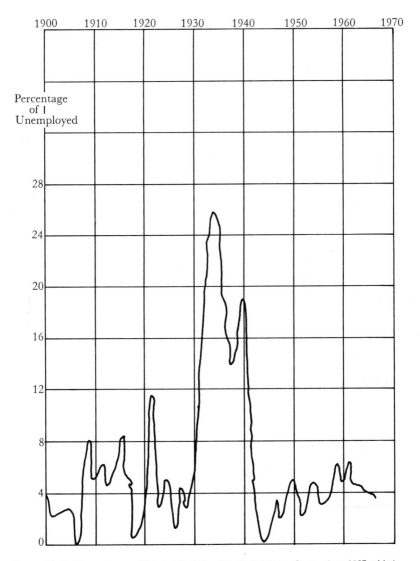

Source: U. S. Census Bureau, *Historical Statistics of the United States;* figures since 1957 added from Morris A. Copland, *Toward Full Employment*, Millard Lectures #7 (New York: Fordham, 1966).

FOOTNOTES

CHAPTER ONE

1. Adrienne Koch and William Peden, eds., *The Life and Selected Writings of Thomas Jefferson* (New York: Modern Library, 1944), p. 714.

2. William Manning, *The Key of Libberty, Showing the Causes Why a Free Government Has Always Failed, and a Remedy Against It*, notes and foreword by Samuel Eliot Morison (Billerica, Mass., 1922), as quoted in Willard Thorp, Merle Curti, and Carlos Baker, eds., *American Issues* (Chicago: J. B. Lippincott, 1955), I:192.

3. Quoted by Henry Adams in Herbert Agar, ed., *The Formative Years: A History of the United States During the Administration of Jefferson and Madison* (Boston: Houghton Mifflin Company, 1947), I:41.

4. Charles Nisbet, *Memoir of the Rev. Charles Nisbet, D. D., Late President of Dickinson College, Carlisle* (New York: Robert Carter, 1840), pp. 268f.

5. *Ibid.*

6. Merle M. Odgers, "Education and the American Philosophical Society," in American Philosophical Society *Proceedings*, LXXXVII (1944):13, 15-18.

7. Samuel Miller, *A Brief Retrospect of the Eighteenth Century*, 2 vols. (New York, 1803).

8. *Ibid.*, II:295f, 299, 441f.

9. *Ibid.*, II:300.

10. *Ibid.*, II:295f, 299, 300f.

11. *Ibid.*, II:271.

12. *Ibid.*, II:273.

13. *Ibid.*, II:43.

14. *Ibid.*, II:286f.

15. Jedidiah Morse, *A Sermon Exhibiting the Present Dangers, and Consequent Duties of the Citizens of the United States of America. Delivered at Charlestown, April 25, 1790, the Day of the National Fast* (Charlestown, 1799), p. 12.

16. Miller, *Brief Retrospect*, II: 441f.

17. *Ibid.*, II:275.

18. Letter from Joseph C. Cabell to Joseph Lancaster, 1 July 1819, as quoted in Edgar W. Knight and Clifton L. Hall, eds., *Readings in American Educational History* (New York: Appleton Century Crofts, 1951), p. 137.

19. Merle Curti, *The Growth of American Thought*, 2nd ed. (New York: Harper and Brothers, 1951), p. 214.

20. Harry R. Warfel, *Noah Webster: Schoolmaster to America* (New York: Macmillan Company, 1936), pp. 339f. Donald G. Tewksbury's *The Founding of American Colleges and Universities Before the Civil War* (New York, 1932) is the definitive work on this subject. See also, Frank Tracy Carlton, *Economic Influences Upon Educational Progress in the United States, 1820-1850* (Madison, Wisconsin, 1908), pp. 19ff, 58ff; Merle Curti, *Social Ideas of American Educators; with New Chapter on the Last Twenty-Five Years* (Paterson: Pageant Books, 1959), pp. 24f.

21. Richard Hofstadter, *Academic Freedom in the Age of the College* (New York: Columbia University Press, 1960), pp. 210f.

22. David Bruce Tyack, "Gentleman of Letters: A Study of George Ticknor" (Doctoral diss., Harvard University, 1958), pp. 66-69.

23. Walter P. Metzger, *Academic Freedom in the Age of the University* (New York: Columbia University Press, 1961), pp. 9-19, *passim*.

24. For detailed studies from which the following information has been essentially derived see

Dumas Malone, *The Public Life of Thomas Cooper* (New Haven, 1926) and Daniel Walker Hollis, *University of South Carolina, I, South Carolina College* (Columbia, S. C., 1951).

25.   Censor, "An Appeal to the State," quoted in Malone, *Thomas Cooper*, p. 339.

26.   *Ibid.*, p. 265.

27.   Hollis, *South Carolina*, I:115.

28.   *Ibid.*, I:161.

29.   *Ibid.*, I:164.

30.   *Ibid.*, I:175.

31.   James Hopkins, *The University of Kentucky* (Lexington, 1951), p. 25.

32.   Robert Davidson, *The History of the Presbyterian Church in Kentucky* (New York, 1847), pp. 284f.

33.   Mattie Austin Hatcher, *Letters of an Early American Traveler, Mary Austin Holley, Her Life and Works, 1784-1846* (Dallas, 1933), p. 17.

34.   Philip Lindsley, *Speech About Colleges Delivered in Nashville on Commencement Day, October 4, 1848* (Nashville, 1848), p. 22.

35.   Lucius S. Merriam, "Higher Education in Tennessee," in Herbert B. Adams, ed., *Contributions to American Educational History*, No. 16 (Washington, 1893), p. 30.

36.   *Ibid.*, p. 19.

CHAPTER TWO

1.   Horace Greeley, *Recollections of a Busy Life* (New York, 1868), p. 527. See an appraisal and analysis of the pre-Civil War reform spirit in Henry Steele Commager, ed., *The Era of Reform, 1830-1860* (Princeton: Anvil Books, 1960), pp. 7-17, *passim*.

2.   Ralph Waldo Emerson, "Man the Reformer," in *Nature Addresses and Lectures* (Boston: Houghton Mifflin Company, 1903), p. 228.

3.   Charles A. Beard, "Historians at Work: Brooks and Henry Adams," in *Atlantic Monthly*, CLXXI (April, 1943):89.

4.   *Barnard's American Journal of Education*, I (1855-56):591, as quoted by Lawrence A. Cremin, *The American Common School: An Historic Conception* (New York: Bureau of Publications, Teachers College, 1951), p. 92.

5.   Louise Hall Tharp, *Until Victory: Horace Mann and Mary Peabody* (Boston: Little, Brown, 1953) is replete with similarly interesting and incidental information.

6.   Mary Peabody Mann, *Life of Horace Mann*, centennial ed. in facsimile (Washington, D. C., National Education Association, 1937), pp. 80, 88.

7.   *Ibid.*, p. 80.

8.   Julian Hawthorne, *Hawthorne and His Circle* (New York: Harper and Bros., 1903), p. 44.

9.   *Ibid.*, pp. 44f.

10.   Mann, *Life of Horace Mann*, p. 142.

11.   *Ibid.*

12.   *Ibid.*

13.   *Ibid.* Emphasis ours.

14.   *Ibid.*, p. 172. For an apt summary of Mann's notion of ideal teacher-training, see Clarence J. Karier's keenly perceptive study of American educational ideas, *Man, Society, and Education* (Glenview, Ill.: Scott, Foresman and Co., 1967), pp. 61-64.

15.   Mann, *Life of Horace Mann*, p. 366.

16.   *Ibid.*

17.   *Ibid.*

18.   *Ibid.*, p. 271.

19.   *Ibid.*, p. 142.

20.   Horace Mann, "The Necessity of Education in a Republican Government," in *Life and Works of Horace Mann*, 5 Vols. (Boston, 1891), II:165f. On this question,

Mann's position is transitional. Not until the eve of the Civil War did popular literature generally reflect a total denial of human depravity or innate wicked propensities. See Bernard Wishy, *The Child and the Republic* (Philadelphia: University of Pennsylvania Press, 1968), p. 22.
21. Mann, "Necessity of Education," p. 187.
22. *Ibid.*
23. Lawrence A. Cremin, "Horace Mann's Legacy," in *The Republic and the School: Horace Mann on the Education of Free Men*, Lawrence A. Cremin, ed. (New York: Bureau of Publications, Teachers College, 1957), p. 13.
24. *Ibid.*, p. 24.
25. Some sources put the date of Maclure's retirement in America at 1799. See J. Percy Moore, "William Maclure—Scientist and Humanitarian," in American Philosophical Society *Proceedings*, XCI (1947):236.
26. Harlow Lindley, ed., *Indiana as Seen by Early Travelers* (Indianapolis: Indiana Historical Commission, 1916), p. 411.
27. William Maclure, *Opinions on Various Subjects, Dedicated to the Industrious Producers*, 2 Vols. (New Harmony, 1831-1837), II: 87. Other editions of *Opinions* are in three-volume sets.
28. *Ibid.*, II:208f.
29. *Ibid.*, I:67.
30. *Working Man's Advocate*, May 29, 1830. Interestingly enough, supporters of Protestant missionary activity among the Indians depended heavily upon the boarding school idea. Indeed, they used Maclurian arguments in hailing the boarding school as "the answer to their prayers" for a suitable method of missionization, Christianization, and Americani-

zation. In the nineteenth century the idea of the boarding school as a model community came "into its own in missionary work." See Robert F. Berkhofer, Jr., "Model Zions for the American Indian," in *American Quarterly*, XV (Summer, 1963):177f, 176-190, *passim.*
31. The point of view that came to dominate his thought on this subject was that "no good system of education can have a fair tryal but with orphans." From time to time, however, he admitted to a hope that properly educated children could bring changes in parental views and values. "The improvement of the child will conduce to a change in the parent, and civilisation be advanced at both ends." His overarching program nonetheless continued to be premised on the gradual transformation of society through universal boarding school education for both sexes. See Arthur E. Bestor, Jr., ed., "Education and Reform at New Harmony; Correspondence of William Maclure and Marie Duclos Fretageot," in Indiana Historical Society *Publications*, XV (1948):301, 308f, 351.
32. See, for example, G. Stanley Hall, "The Fall of Atlantis," in *Recreations of a Psychologist* (New York, 1920), pp. 1-127; B. F. Skinner, *Walden Two* (New York, 1948).
33. Maclure, *Opinions*, II:207.
34. *Ibid.*, II:346f.
35. *Ibid.*, I:72.
36. *Ibid.*, I:25.
37. *Ibid.*, I:70, 72.
38. *Ibid.*, I:106.
39. *Ibid.*, II:458, 467.
40. *Ibid.*, I:62; Bestor, "Education and Reform," p. 294.
41. Maclure, *Opinions*, I:95, 184, II:211f; Bestor, "Education and Reform," p. 389.

42. Cited by Will S. Monroe, *The History of the Pestalozzian Movement in the United States* (Syracuse, 1907), pp. 51f, 58, 110f. In line with practices of such reformers as Emmanuel Fellenberg, products of student labor were sold or consumed locally to help defray school costs.
43. Bestor, "Education and Reform," p. 306.
44. Maclure, *Opinions*, II:102f.
45. *Ibid.*, I:57.
46. *Ibid.*, I:57f, 81.
47. *Ibid.*, II:287.
48. *Ibid.* In 1822 Maclure told scientist Benjamin Silliman of Yale, "In reflecting upon the absurdity of my own classical education, launched into the world as ignorant as a pig of anything useful . . . , I had been long in the habit of considering education one of the greatest abuses our species were guilty of. . . ." Bestor, "Education and Reform," p. 293.
49. Maclure, *Opinions*, I:394, II: 303f, 361, 513, 524, 545-549. Maclure's denunciation of history echoed Voltaire's charge that "the history of great events in the world is scarcely more than a history of crimes." See Carl Becker, *The Heavenly City of the Eighteenth Century Philosophers* (New Haven, 1961), p. 93.
50. Maclure, *Opinions*, II:209, 508. Emphasis ours.
51. *Ibid.*, I:93f.
52. *Ibid.*, II:100.
53. *Ibid.*, II:102f, 99-103.
54. *Ibid.*, II:309.
55. *Ibid.*, I:42, II:163.
56. *Ibid.*, II:154, 301f.
57. Frances Trollope, *Domestic Manners of the Americans*, Donald Smalley, ed. (New York, 1960), pp. xx, xxi, 10ff.
58. Mary Turner Carriel, *The Life of Jonathan Baldwin Turner* (Urbana: University of Illinois Press, 1961), p. xi.
59. *Ibid.*, p. 114. By his allusion to "military classes" Turner reminded his contemporaries that the Federal Government had already seen fit to serve the interests of warfare with its establishment of West Point. Surely the government could do no less than lend like support to peaceful educational objectives of a free people as well. "Has God so made the world that peculiar schools, peculiar applications of science, and a peculiar resultant literature are found indispensable to the highest success in the art of killing men, in all states, while nothing of the kind can be based on the infinitely multifarious arts and processes of feeding, clothing, and housing them?" *Ibid.*, pp. 106f.
60. Jonathan Baldwin Turner, "Plan for an Industrial University for the State of Illinois," in *The University Studies*, Vol. IV, No. 1 (Urbana-Champaign, Illinois: University Press, November, 1910), 69.
61. Carriel, *Jonathan Baldwin Turner*, p. 113.
62. *Ibid.*, p. 112.
63. *Ibid.*, pp. 114, 162.
64. *Ibid.*, p. 226.
65. *Ibid.*, p. 66
66. Turner, "Plan for an Industrial University," p. 66.
67. *Ibid.*, p. 67.
68. *Ibid.*, p. 79.
69. *Ibid.*, p. 69.
70. *Ibid.*, p. 80.
71. *Ibid.*, p. 76. Clearly President James Buchanan missed the significant returns such institutions could make to the nation as a whole. When, in 1859, he vetoed a bill essentially the same as the Morrill Bill, which Lincoln signed

into law three years later, Buchanan portrayed the federal government as a "prudent proprietor of land." Seen in this light, the government was justified in promoting education through Northwest Ordinances because they promoted broader national interests, i.e., westward migration and the sale of public lands. Using this principle Buchanan explained his veto of the "Bill Donating Public Lands." "No person will contend that donations of land to all the States of the Union for the erection of colleges within the limits of each can be embraced by this principle. It cannot be pretended that an agricultural college in New York or Virginia would aid the settlement or facilitate the sale of public lands in Minnesota or California. This cannot possibly be embraced within the authority which a prudent proprietor of land would exercise over his own possessions." John Bassett Moore, ed., *The Works of James Buchanan* (New York: Antiquarian Press, Ltd., 1960), X:309. Ironically, the Morrill Act, to an impressive extent, satisfied the pinched and restrictive principle Buchanan applied in his veto message. For a helpful appraisal of the historical relations between the colleges and public interest and the "land grab" *versus* "land grant" controversy see Theodore R. Crane, ed., "To Build an American University," in *The Colleges and the Public, 1787-1862* (New York: Bureau of Publications, Teachers College, Columbia University, 1963), pp. 1-33.

72. Turner, "Plan for an Industrial University," p. 78.
73. *Ibid.*, p. 79.
74. *Ibid.*, p. 75.
75. *Ibid.*, p. 76. Emphasis ours.

76. *Ibid.*, pp. 70f.
77. *Ibid.*, pp. 83f.
78. "Secular" is here used in the sense of "public and dependent on illustration, argument, and evidence having reasonably clear referents in the empirical order." It is used with reference to what Walter Metzger called "the formula for tolerating error" in the post-Darwinian attitude toward academic freedom: "To them, all beliefs are tentatively true or tentatively false, and only verifiable through a continuous process of inquiry...."
"The evolutionist's formula did not level every opinion to equal value. It held that every claim to a discovery of truth must submit to open verification; that the process of verification must follow certain rules; that this procedure is best understood by those who qualify as experts. Hence, academic freedom does not theoretically justify all kinds of intellectual nonconformity, but only that kind of nonconformity that proceeds according to rules; not any private belief, but that kind of private belief that allows itself publicly to be tested...." Richard Hofstadter and Walter P. Metzger, *The Development of Academic Freedom in the United States* (New York: Columbia University Press, 1955), p. 364.
79. James Bryce, *University and Historic Addresses* (New York, 1913), p. 170.
80. *Ibid.*, p. 163.
81. Frederick Jackson Turner, *The Frontier in American History* (New York, 1920), p. 283.
82. Norman Foerster, *The American State University* (Chapel Hill, 1937), p. 3.
83. Turner, *Frontier*, p. 283.
84. *Ibid.*, p. 284.

85. Lawrence A. Cremin, "The Future of the American Common School," in *Public Education in America,* George Z. F. Bereday and Luigi Volpicelli, eds. (New York: Harper and Brothers, 1958), p. 46.

CHAPTER THREE
1. Horace Mann, "What God Does, and What He Leaves for Man to Do, in the Work of Education," in *Life and Works of Horace Mann* (Boston: Lee and Shepard Publishers, 1891), II:216.
2. Henry Seidel Canby, *The Age of Confidence* (New York: Farrar and Rinehart, 1934), pp. 110f. If the decade of the 1890's was filled with sham and corruption, Canby mused, it was also remembered as a historic terminus, when "for the last time in living memory everyone knew exactly what it meant to be an American." *Ibid.,* p. 6.
3. Finley Peter Dunne, *Mr. Dooley in Peace and In War* (Boston: Small, Maynard and Co., 1899), p. 125.
4. William Graham Sumner, *Selected Essays of William Graham Sumner,* Stow Persons, ed. and intro. (Englewood Cliffs N.J.: Prentice Hall, Inc., 1963), p. 179.
5. Boyd H. Bode, "William James in the American Tradition," in Max C. Otto *et. al., William James: The Man and the Thinker* (Madison: University of Wisconsin Press, 1942), p. 109.
6. William James, *The Will to Believe* (n.p.; Dover Publications Inc., n.d.), p. 99.
7. Quoted by John Dewey, "William James and the World Today," in Otto, *William James,* p. 92.
8. James, *Will,* p. 169.
9. Merle Curti, *The Social Ideas of American Educators,* rev. ed. (Pat-

erson: Littlefield, Adams and Co., 1959), p. 325.
10. W. T. Harris to S. S. Mc-Clure, Esquire, Sept. 7, 1887, Item no. 863, container no. 47, William T. Harris Manuscript Collection, Library of Congress. Hereafter referred to as "WTH Collection."
11. Jean Jacques Rousseau, *Emile,* Barbara Foxley, tr. (London: J. M. Dent and Sons, n.d.), p. 1.
12. "My C Supts Address," Item no. 28, container no. 2. WTH Collection. (Found loose therein as part of five-page item pinned together.)
13. *Ibid.*
14. Quoted by Gordon C. Lee, *Education and Democratic Ideals* (New York: Harcourt, Brace and World, Inc., 1965), p. 136.
15. William T. Harris, "The Science of Education," in *Journal of Speculative Philosophy,* XIII (1879): 211.
16. William T. Harris, "Elementary School Education," in *Journal of Speculative Philosophy,* III (1869): 185ff.
17. Quoted by B. Holmes, "Some Writings of William T. Harris," in *British Journal of Educational Studies,* V (1956):61.
18. William T. Harris, "Do the Public Schools Educate Children Beyond the Position Which They Must Occupy in Life?" in *Report,* Connecticut Board of Education, 1882, p. 50. Item no. 29, container no. 2, WTH Collection.
19. Ralph Barton Perry, *The Thought and Character of William James,* 2 vols. (Boston: Little, Brown and Co., 1935), I:742, 753.
20. George B. Lockwood, *The New Harmony Movement,* William T. Harris, intro. (New York: D. Appleton and Co., 1905) p. xii.
21. Lancelot Law Whyte, *The*

Unconscious Before Freud (Garden City: Anchor Books, 1962), p. 155.
22. See Edward L. Thorndike, "Biographical Memoir of Granville Stanley Hall, 1844-1924," in *Biographical Memoirs*, National Academy of Science, XII (1928): 161-180, *passim.*
23. G. Stanley Hall, *Life and Confessions of a Psychologist* (New York: D. Appleton and Co., 1923), p. 596.
24. Quoted by Thorndike, "Biographical Memoir," p. 147; S. C. Fisher, "The Psychological and Educational Work of Granville Stanley Hall," in *American Journal of Psychology* XXXVI (1925): 49f.
25. Quoted by Lorine Pruette, *G. Stanley Hall: A Biography of a Mind* (New York: D. Appleton and Co., 1926), p. 7.
26. *Ibid.*, p. 181 *et passim.*
27. Josiah Royce, *Lectures on Modern Idealism* (New Haven: Yale University Press, 1919), pp. 236f.
28. Hall, *Life*, pp. 15, 16, 445.
29. Hall, "Editorial," in *Pedagogical Seminary*, I(1891):120.
30. *Ibid.*, pp. 124f.
31. William T. Harris, "Excessive Helps in Education," in *Education*, IX (December, 1888):215-220, *passim;* Harris, "Relation of the Art to the Science of Education," in *Proceedings*, National Educational Association, Part II (Madison, 1884):190-194, *passim,* III:56f.
32. *Ibid.;* Curti, *Social Ideas*, Ch. IX, *passim.*
33. See *Proceedings*, National Educational Association (Saratoga Springs, 1885), pp. 504f.
34. *Ibid.* (Minneapolis, 1902), pp. 270ff.
35. Hall, "Moral Education and Will-Training," in *Pedagogical Seminary*, II (1892):86. Hall had published essentially the same article

at least twice earlier—in 1882, in the *American Institute of Instruction* (Boston), pp. 236-271, and in the *Princeton Review*, X:306-325.
36. Hall, "Moral Education and Will-Training," p. 86.
37. Hall, "Editorial," in *Pedagogical Seminary*, II (1892):4.
38. Hall, "Child Study as a Basis for Psychology and Psychological Teaching," in *Proceedings*, International Congress of Education of the World's Columbian Exposition, Chicago, July 25-28, 1893 (New York, 1894), pp. 717f.
39. Hall, "Moral Education and Will-Training," p. 88.
40. Hall, "Recreation and Reversion," in *Pedagogical Seminary*, XXII (1915):510-520, *passim.* War in Europe prevented Hall from reading this paper in Leipzig.
41. Hall, "The Education of Ministers and Sunday School Work Among the Unitarians," in *Pedagogical Seminary*, XII (1905):491.
42. Hall, *Educational Problems*, 2 vols. (New York: D. Appleton and Co., 1911), II:667. By permission of Appleton-Century, affiliate of Meredith Press. Copyright, 1911, by D. Appleton & Company. Copyright renewed, 1939, by Robert Granville Hall.
43. Hall, "Moral Education and Will-Training," p. 77.
44. Hall, "The Moral and Religious Training of Children," in *Journal of Social Science*, XV (February, 1882):66 *et seq.* Hall believed that "men were mistaken when they thought they had done well in raising God from that region where he is clung to by the whole soul with all its spontaneous energy, and conferring on him the honor of exactly demonstrating his existence." *Ibid.*, p. 68.
45. *Ibid.*, pp. 65ff, 70f. See also

Proceedings, National Educational Association (Madison, 1884), III: 48, in which Hall made an early declaration of his lifelong belief that "The aim of education should be to teach the subordination of self to the good of society."
46. Hall, "Moral Education and Will-Training," pp. 79f.
47. *Ibid.*, p. 82. Hall did add that flogging should be administered only with discretion.
48. Hall, *Educational Problems*, II:628. The word *Dressur*, more commonly used with reference to animals than to humans, describes the training of a creature to practice habitual, prompt obedience.
49. Hall, "The Ideal School as Based on Child Study," in *Proceedings*, National Educational Association (Detroit, 1901), pp. 482, 474-488 *passim*.
50. *New York Tribune*, V:1 (February 5, 1905).
51. Hall, "Moral Education and Will-Training," pp. 74f.
52. Hall, "Child Study: The Basis of Exact Education," in *Forum*, XVI (December, 1893):436.
53. *Ibid.*: Hall, "Editorial," in *Pedagogical Seminary*, II(1892):7f.
54. Hall, "Moral Education and Will-Training," pp. 84f.
55. Hall, "The Pedagogy of History," in *Pedagogical Seminary*, XII (1905):347. See also *Educational Problems*, II:Ch. XIV, *passim*.
56. Hall, "Moral Education and Will-Training," p. 75.
57. Hall, "Editorial," II:7f.
58. Hall, *Educational Problems*, II:605; Hall, "The Educational State," p. 719; Hall, "Editorial," II:189; Hall, "Certain Degenerative Tendencies Among Teachers," in *Pedagogical Seminary*, XII (1905):460f.
59. Hall, "Clouds," in *Pedagogical Seminary*, IX (1902):506.

60. Hall, "The Ideal School as Based on Child Study," p. 481. Hall listed the composer Wagner as the author of one of the ten greatest "books" of the nineteenth century, because Wagner had "reedited the myths which constitute the best part of the ethnic Bible of his race and brought them home to the heart . . . " through his music. Hall, "The Greatest Books of the Century," in *Outlook*, LXVI (December 1, 1900):799f. For a cogent discussion of Wagner's place in nineteenth-century German culture see Jacques Barzun, *Darwin, Marx, Wagner: Critique of a Heritage*, 2d ed., rev. (Garden City, 1958), part iii, pp. 231-320.
61. Hall, "The Ideal School as Based on Child Study," p. 483. Plato's stories of the Cave and the Two Steeds were recommended by Hall.
62. Hall, "Educational Reforms," in *Pedagogical Seminary*, I (1891): 11f. For Hall's Children's Institute plans see his *Life*, pp. 390-405.
63. Hall, "Educational Reforms," pp. 10ff.
64. Hall, "Certain Degenerative Tendencies," pp. 461ff; Hall, "The Ideal School as Based on Child Study," pp. 484ff; Hall, *Adolescence: Its Psychology and its Relations to Physiology, Anthropology, Sociology, Sex, Crime, Religion and Education*, 2 vols. (New York, 1904).
65. Hall emphatically wanted male teachers in his schools. He frequently attacked the feminization of the teaching profession. Women would not flog; they clucked motheringly over dullards and ignored better students; they were incapable of administering *dressur;* and they made a boy effeminate during their reign of "sugary benignity." Hall, *Educa-*

tional Problems, II:582 *et seq.*

66. Hall, "Coeducation in the High School," in *Proceedings,* National Education Association (Boston, 1903), pp. 446-451; Hall, "Coeducation," in *Proceedings,* National Education Association (St. Louis, 1904), pp. 538-452.

67. Hall, *Educational Problems,* II:586.

68. Hall, "Certain Degenerative Tendencies," p. 462.

69. Hall, "New Ideals of Motherhood Suggested by Child Study," in *Report of the National Congress of Mothers,* IX (Washington, D. C., March 10-17, 1905):14, 18.

70. Hall, *Educational Problems,* II:636.

71. *Ibid.,* Ch. XXIII, *passim;* Hall, "The High School as the People's College versus the Fitting School," in *Pedagogical Seminary,* IX (1902): 63-73, *passim; Report of the Committee of Ten on Secondary School Studies—With the Reports of the Conferences Arranged by the Committee* (New York, 1894), pp. 17, 39, 51f. The committee did assert, however, that secondary schools "do not exist for the purpose of preparing boys and girls for colleges." *Ibid.,* pp. 51f. For a brief, incisive appraisal of the work of the Committee and for the reaction of its chairman, Harvard President Charles W. Eliot, to Hall's attacks see *Charles W. Eliot and Popular Education,* Edward A. Krug, ed. (New York, 1961), pp. 7-16, 19f, 83-99, 147-166.

72. Hall, "Adolescents and High School English, Latin, and Algebra," in *Pedagogical Seminary,* IX (1902):100 *et seq.*

73. Hall, *Educational Problems,* II:646.

74. *Ibid.,* II:650.

75. Hall, "The Ideal School as Based on Child Study," p. 484.

76. Hall, "Child Study: The Basis of Exact Education," p. 439.

77. Hall, "Vigorous Attack on Classics," in *Journal of Education,* LXVI (July 4, 1907):34; Hall, *Educational Problems,* II:652f. After World War I Hall "readmitted" Latin on the condition that it be taught for its morale-building tales, not for bilingualism. Hall, *Morale: The Supreme Standard of Life and Conduct* (New York: D. Appleton and Co., 1920), Ch. XVII, *passim.*

78. Hall, *Educational Problems,* II:653, 660; Ch. XV, *passim.*

79. *Ibid.,* II:618, 622.

80. *Ibid.,* II:676, 682.

81. *Ibid.,* II:630, 675.

82. Hall, "Certain Degenerative Tendencies," p. 459.

83. Hall, *Educational Problems,* II:655-658; Hall, "The High School as the People's College," pp. 63-73, *passim.*

84. *Ibid.,* pp. 68ff.

85. Hall, *Educational Problems,* II:659. See also Hall, *Life,* pp. 518f.

86. Hall, "The High School as the People's College," pp. 69 *et seq;* Hall, *Educational Problems,* II:661; Hall, *Life,* pp. 518f.

87. Nietzsche, however, took exception to the myths Wagner created. *Parsifal's* appearance as a new Christ figure disgusted Nietzsche while it won the applause of Hall. See Barzun, *Darwin, Marx, Wagner,* pp. 231-320.

88. Hall, "Pedagogy of History," pp. 343f.

89. Hall, "Moral Education and Will-Training," pp. 84ff.

90. Hall, *Life,* pp. 147ff, 194f.

91. Hall, *Educational Problems,* II:643.

92. *Ibid.,* II:642f.

93. Charles E. Strickland and Charles Burgess, eds., *Health,*

Growth, and Heredity: G. Stanley Hall on Natural Education (New York: Teachers College Press, 1965), p. viii. For all its benignity, Hall's sense of community and education represents the closest anticipatory approximation of national socialism to be expounded in America. See, for example, George L. Mosse, *Nazi Culture* (New York: Grosset and Dunlap, 1966).

CHAPTER FOUR

1. G. Stanley Hall, *Life and Confessions of a Psychologist* (New York: D. Appleton and Co., 1923), p. 222.
2. Quoted by John Dewey, *German Philosophy and Politics* (New York, 1915), pp. 21ff, 27.
3. See Johann Gottlieb Fichte, *Addresses to the German Nation* (Chicago, 1922), *passim;* Herbert Spencer, *Principles of Psychology,* 2 vols. (New York, 1873), I:614-628; *Rousseau's Emile: or Treatise on Education,* William H. Payne, tr. (New York, 1908), pp. 22, 52ff, 135; and Hall, *Founders of Modern Psychology* (New York, 1912), pp. 198-240.
4. Hall, *Jesus, the Christ, in the Light of Psychology,* 2 vols. (Garden City: Doubleday, Page and Co., 1917). These volumes contain Hall's major exposition on the Christ-like superman.
5. Hall, *Life,* p. 223.
6. *Ibid.,* pp. 35 *et seq.,* 575f.
7. Hall, "The Moral and Religious Training of Children," in *Journal of Social Science,* XV (February, 1882):56f.
8. *Ibid.,* 57ff.
9. Hall, "Educational Reforms," in *Pedagogical Seminary,* I(1891):2.
10. Hall, "The Educational State or the Methods of Education in

Europe," in *Christian Register,* LXIX (November 6, 1890):719; Hall, "New Departures in Education," in *North American Review,* CXL(1885):148.
11. Hall, "The Fall of Atlantis," in *Recreations of a Psychologist* (New York: D. Appleton and Co., 1920), pp. 1-127.
12. *Ibid.,* pp. 45-70 *passim.*
13. *Ibid.,* pp. 78ff.
14. *Ibid.,* p. 82.
15. *Ibid.,* p. 71.
16. John Dewey, *Lectures in the Philosophy of Education: 1899.* Reginald D. Archambault, ed. and intro. (New York: Random House, 1966), pp. 286, 187-197 *passim.*
17. Dewey, *The Public and Its Problems* (Denver: Alan Swallow, 1927), p. 98.
18. *Ibid.*
19. James T. Farrell *et al., Dialogue on John Dewey,* Corliss Lamont, ed. (New York: Horizon Press, 1959), p. 90. Quoted by Herbert Schneider.
20. *Ibid.,* p. 88. Quoted by James T. Farrell.
21. *Dewey on Education,* Martin Dworkin, ed. (New York: Teachers College Press, 1958), p. 111.
22. Dewey, *Impressions of Soviet Russia and the Revolutionary World* (New York: New Republic, Inc., 1929), p. 32. These impressions appeared originally as articles in the *New Republic.*
23. *Ibid.,* pp. 40, 105-108.
24. Hall, *Life,* pp. 439f. Emphasis added.
25. Hall, *Morale,* pp. 328, 337.
26. Hall, *Life,* p. 535.
27. Hall, *Morale,* pp. 331, 333.
28. Dewey, *Human Nature and Conduct* (New York: Henry Holt and Co., 1922), pp. 293f.
29. Dewey, *Impressions,* pp. 31, 59, 116. These observations are weakened as evidence if one con-

cludes that they are merely un-studied reactions and truly "impressions." On the other hand, one might take special note of these observations precisely because they are unstudied and unguardedly straightforward.

30. Farrell, *Dialogue*, p. 124, e.g.

31. Dewey, *Impressions*, p. 86. Emphasis added.

32. *Ibid.*, p. 121.

33. Dewey, "Critique of American Civilization," in *Recent Gains in American Civilization*, Kirby Page, ed. (Chautauqua: The Chautauqua Press, 1928), pp. 256f. 271f.

34. Dewey, *Liberalism and Social Action* (New York: Capricorn Books, 1963), pp. 89f.

35. Dewey, *Individualism Old and New* (New York: Capricorn Books, 1962), pp. 164f.

36. Dewey, *Public*, p. 167.

37. *Ibid.*, p. 177.

38. Arthur G. Wirth, *John Dewey as Educator* (New York: John Wiley and Sons, 1966), p. 287.

39. *Ibid.*, p. 297.

40. Dewey, *Philosophy of Education* (New York: Philosophical Library, 1956), p. 66.

41. *Ibid.*, p. 51.

42. *Ibid.*, p. 71. Emphasis added.

43. *Ibid.*, p. 72.

44. *Ibid.*, p. 53.

45. For a trenchant study of Progressivism in American education, see Lawrence A. Cremin, *The Transformation of the School* (New York: A. A. Knopf, 1962); see also Raymond Callahan, *Education and the Cult of Efficiency* (Chicago: University of Chicago Press, 1962).

46. Countless pamphlets, magazines, and books play the same general theme of Dewey and educational conspiracy. See, e.g., John A. Stormer, *None Dare Call It Treason* (Florissant, Mo.: Liberty Bell Press, 1964), esp. ch. VI. This volume was widely circulated during the Johnson-Goldwater Presidential campaign in 1964.

47. Charles Frankel, "John Dewey's Legacy," in *American Scholar*, 29(Summer, 1960):313.

CHAPTER FIVE

1. See Chart I, p. 138.

2. John D. Durand, *The Labor Force in the United States* (Washington: Social Science Research Council, 1948), p. 66.

3. See Chart II, p. 139.

4. See Chart III, p. 140.

5. See Chart IV, p. 141.

6. Cf. Educational Policies Commission, *Manpower and Education* (Washington: National Education Association, 1956), Chapter II.

7. For the early years of the efficiency movement see Samuel Haber, *Efficiency and Uplift* (Chicago: University of Chicago Press, 1964).

8. Raymond Callahan, *Education and the Cult of Efficiency* (Chicago: University of Chicago Press, 1962) provides the best general treatment of the efficiency movement particularly with respect to school administration. For his treatment of the Gary system see pp. 128-147. For background on the social efficiency movement in education in the early decades see Edward Krug, *The Shaping of the American High School* (New York: Harpers, 1964).

9. CF. Walter Drost, *David Snedden and Education for Social Efficiency* (Madison, Wisconsin: University of Wisconsin Press, 1967).

10. Randolph Bourne, "The Twilight of the Idols," *Untimely Papers* (New York: B. W. Huebsch, 1919).

11. See The National Manpower Council, *Education and Manpower*, Henry David, ed. (New York: Columbia University Press, 1960) for an overview of the general sense of urgency about manpower problems; Cf., Jerry M. Rosenberg, *Automation, Manpower, and Education* (New York: Random House, 1966).

12. One can see both continuity and response to novelty in the humanist educational critic in the following sampling of sources: Irving Babbitt, *Literature and the American College* (Boston: Houghton Mifflin, 1908); Robert M. Hutchins, *The Higher Learning in America* (New Haven: Yale University Press, 1936); Norman Foerster, *The American State University* . . . (Chapel Hill: University of North Carolina Press, 1937); Albert Lynd, *Quackery in the Public Schools* (Boston: Atlantic Monthly Press, 1950); Arthur Bestor, *Educational Wastelands* (Urbana: University of Illinois Press, 1953); and Mortimer Smith, *The Diminished Mind* (Chicago: Henry Regnery, 1954).

13. For a sample of this literature see Council for Basic Education, *A Decade of Comment on Education, 1956-1966*, Mortimer Smith, ed. (Washington: Council for Basic Education, 1966).

14. For a perception of Conant as a person see Merle Borrowman, "Conant, The Man," *Saturday Review*, 46:58-60 (September 21, 1963).

15. James B. Conant, *Public Education and the Structure of American Society* (New York: Teachers College Bureau of Publications, 1946). Conant's most recent books tend to be largely filled with recommendations for action. This applies to *The American High School Today* (New York: McGraw-Hill, 1958); to *The Education of American Teachers* (New York: McGraw-Hill, 1963); and to *Shaping Educational Policy* (New York: McGraw-Hill, 1964). Of the books in which he most clearly defines his own educational values the most recent is *The Child, The Parent, and The State* (Cambridge: Harvard University Press, 1959). This volume particularly shows his own sensitivity to the relationship between educational proposals and the social-economic-political conditions in which a nation finds itself. It also reveals a sense of urgency in the face of conditions then prevailing. *Education and the Divided World* (Cambridge: Harvard University Press, 1949), is a similarly thoughtful book written a decade earlier. His other somewhat more "philosophical" works include *Education and Liberty* (Cambridge: Harvard University Press, 1953) and *The Citadel of Learning* (New Haven: Yale University Press, 1956). The latter, concerning higher education, uses throughout rhetoric that we are compelled to place on the consummatory end of our continuum.

16. See, e.g., James B. Conant, "Education for the Learned Professions," in *Higher Education and Modern Democracy* (New York: Rand McNally, 1967), p. 152.

17. Hyman G. Rickover, *Education and Freedom* (New York: E. P. Dutton, 1959) is largely a set of speeches on educational issues; his *American Education—A National Failure* (New York: E. P. Dutton, 1963) is made up largely of testimony before congressional committees. His other works on education compare his perceptions of European (Swiss and English) and

American schools.
18. Panel on Educational Research and Development, *Innovation and Experiment in Education, A Progress Report of the Panel on Educational Research and Development to the U.S. Commissioner of Education, The director of the National Science Foundation, and the Special Assistant to the President for Science and Technology* (Washington, D. C. U. S. Government Printing Office, 1964). The foreword was written by Zacharias, and we suspect the introduction was also. If so, the language on page 7 sounds signifi-

cantly oriented toward consummatory values, as we have defined them. For example, "The Panel sees no need to ask what field of knowledge is of most worth. Music is important as well as science and both science and music can be sources of pleasure as well as of livelihood."
19. *Ibid.*, for a brief description of some of the "new curriculum" projects. A more complete description of the major projects is available in John Goodlad, *et al., The Changing School Curriculum* (New York: Fund for the Advancement of Education, 1966).